A Gathering of Fugitives

THE WORKS OF LIONEL TRILLING

UNIFORM EDITION

LIONEL TRILLING

A GATHERING OF FUGITIVES

New York and London
HARCOURT BRACE JOVANOVICH
1956

First published in 1956

Copyright © 1956 by Lionel Trilling

Copyright 1955 by the American Academy of Arts and Letters; copyright 1953 by Intercultural Publications, Inc.; copyright 1949, 1950, 1977 by The New Yorker Magazine, Inc.; copyright 1949, 1977 by The New York Times Company; copyright 1952 by *Partisan Review;* copyright 1952, 1953, 1954, 1955, 1956 by The Readers' Subscription, Inc.

Library of Congress Cataloging in Publication Data

Trilling, Lionel, 1905–1975.
A gathering of fugitives.

(The works of Lionel Trilling)
I. Title.   III.   Series: Trilling, Lionel, 1905–1975.
The works of Lionel Trilling.
PS3539.R56G3   1978   809   77–17318
ISBN 0–15–134582–1

B C D E

To Elliot E. Cohen

Acknowledgments

"The Great-Aunt of Mr. Forster," "In Defense of Zola," "A Ramble on Graves," "The Dickens of Our Day," "Edmund Wilson: A Backward Glance," "Two Notes on David Riesman," "Profession: Man of the World," "Adams at Ease," "The Novel Alive or Dead," "Criticism and Aesthetics," and " 'That Smile of Parmenides Made Me Think' " first appeared in *The Griffin*. I thank Mr. Gilman Kraft for permission to reprint them. "A Novel in Passing" and "Dr. Leavis and the Moral Tradition" appeared in *The New Yorker*; "Freud's Last Book" in *The New York Times Book Review*; "The Situation of the American Intellectual at the Present Time" in a shorter version in *Partisan Review* and in the present version in *Perspectives*; "On Not Talking" in the *Proceedings* of the American Academy of Arts and Letters and the National Institute of Arts and Letters; "The Morality of Inertia" in *Great Moral Dilemmas* (Harper and Brothers, 1956) and in *The London Magazine*, having first been read in a lecture series of the Institute for Religious and Social Studies. I am grateful to the editors, publishers, and institutions by whose permission they appear here.

Preface

IN THE preface to a collection of critical writings the author commonly undertakes to identify the principle that binds the separate pieces together into a unity. So far as I am aware, there is no such principle in this volume—there is no unity to it. I think of its contents as being what used to be called fugitive essays. The old name seems appropriate even though it has never been clear to me just what fugitive essays were fleeing from. Perhaps it was unity.

The greater number of these essays first appeared in *The Griffin*, the little monthly magazine of The Readers' Subscription. When Mr. Gilman Kraft organized The Readers' Subscription, he invited Mr. Auden, Mr. Barzun, and me to serve as its editors. Our job was to select a monthly book and write about it in *The Griffin*. Our writing, it turned out, was to be done under conditions which are exceptional and very agreeable. We can assume an audience that really likes books and needs them. They like fiction when they can believe it is not ephemeral, they like poetry, they like biography, and collected letters, and essays, and philosophy. To such an audience one doesn't propose a book by superlatives or by obscuring what faults it may have. One simply undertakes to communicate its interest by speaking of the interest it has for oneself. I, for one, found that this led me to write less formally than I usually do, and more personally, even autobiographically. Writing frequently and regularly for the same audience relaxes the manner of address, and certainly the elaborations and the rigorousness that might be proper for an essay in a quarterly review would have been out of place in this sort of communication, which seemed to me to require a degree of familiarity that modern conditions of writing do not ordinarily encourage.

The predominance in number of the *Griffin* essays sets the tone of this book, and the other pieces have been chosen as being more or less consonant with them. There is one exception, the essay called "The Situation of the American Intellectual at the Present Time." This is the longest and most nearly polemical essay in the book. It was written first as a contribution to the *Partisan Review* symposium, "Our Country and Our Culture," and then expanded to its present length at the invitation of the editor of the third issue of *Perspectives*. One reason I reprint it now is that it has aroused antagonism in some quarters and has frequently been misrepresented, often by quotation out of context. Because I want the essay to be read as written, I have not revised it except to omit two or three inessential sentences and to correct an inaccurate reference to a person. Nor have I revised the other pieces beyond correcting some infelicities of prose, but I have sometimes deleted short passages and I have restored others that, in first publication, had to be omitted for lack of space.

1956   L. T.

Contents

Contents

A Gathering of Fugitives

The Great-Aunt of Mr. Forster

E M. FORSTER has written the biography of his great-aunt. It sounds odd as one says it; it rings with the enchanted precision of a French exercise. *Voici la vie de ma grand'tante, dit le grand écrivain anglais.* Marianne Thornton was the sister of Mr. Forster's paternal grandmother. In what way was she notable above other women? So far as deeds go, she is likely to be remembered for only one, an act of public beneficence. When she died, at the age of ninety, she left her grandnephew £8,000, and this, as he says, made possible his career as a writer. It is with the recording of this legacy that Mr. Forster brings his book about Marianne Thornton to a close, as if it were the crown of her life, as indeed it is.

Gautier said of his friend Flaubert that part of his creative endowment was the comfortable income which he had inherited from his father. Americans, always a little hoity-toity about money, and inclined to suppose that cash and "spiritual values," especially art, are ever at war with each other, might be led to think that Gautier was speaking ironically. Nothing could have been further from his intention. He had, poor man, experienced all too much financial exigency, he knew all too well what effect the lack of money has upon the management of a talent, to be anything but simple in his remark. He knew that to a writer money means peace and the opportunity to take thought. There are, no doubt, writers who do not need or want peace and the opportunity to take thought, but Mr. Forster is not one of these. And although his life of his great-aunt is, for several reasons, very heavily charged with irony, there is only the simplest piety of gratitude as he speaks of her bequest to him.

This £8,000 has been the financial salvation of my life. Thanks to it, I was able to go to Cambridge—impossible otherwise, for I failed to win scholarships. After Cambridge I was able to travel for a couple of years, and travelling inclined me to write. After my first visit to India and after the First World War the value of the £8,000 began to diminish, and later on it practically vanished. But by then my writings had begun to sell, and I have been able to live on them instead. Whether—in so stormy an age as ours—this is a reputable sequence I do not know. Still less do I know how the sequence and all sequences will end, with the storms increasing. But I am thankful so far, and thankful to Marianne Thornton; for she and no one else made my career as a writer possible, and her love, in a most tangible sense, followed me beyond the grave.

One is sorry that the £8,000 has vanished, not only for Mr. Forster's sake but for the sake of the money itself—it was such good *old* money, and it had a good deal of tradition attached to it. It got its start early in the eighteenth century in the Russian trade and then went into banking. It was more or less the kind of money that W. B. Yeats liked to think he was connected with when he wasn't keeping in mind his presumed relationship with the Duke of Ormonde—money and blood are always very close to each other, and Yeats took pleasure in saying that his blood came from the loins of men who made their money in one way and not in another, from the loins of "merchants," not of "hucksters." In the heyday of such feelings Dickens meditated on the mystery of a brewer's natural social superiority to a baker. The answer, of course, is that in these things largeness is all—had there been wax-paper to permit loaves to attain a national rather than a local distribution, a baker would have had as much chance of a peerage as a brewer. Then there was the matter of personal service: to *wait upon* a customer in a Shop was degrading almost beyond redemption by prosperity, and in 1882 Marianne Thornton was in despair and called in the family lawyers because the widow of a favorite nephew undertook to marry a Mr. Aylworth; he was a well-to-do man, and a good man, and an excellent musician, but he kept a Shop.

The Thorntons had been in finance for nearly a century before Marianne was born. They had been an ecclesiastical family until the end of the seventeenth century, at which time they shifted their talents from the Church to the City and made money for generations. Robert Thornton, great-grandfather of Marianne, was a director of the Bank of England and it was he who, in 1735, settled the family on what was to become its native heath, Clapham. His son John duplicated his father's career, but added certain intellectual and religious features. He was a friend of William Cowper, and of Cowper's Rev. John Newton, and he established the family in the Evangelicism which became one of its chief characteristics. Marianne's father, Henry, was John's younger son. He too was a banker.

But he was a good deal more than that, and had he been my great-grandfather, I think I should have been more open in my admiration than Mr. Forster is. For example, I should have done as much by him as the Dictionary of National Biography does in perpetuating John Stuart Mill's handsome compliment to his *Enquiry into the Nature and Effects of the Paper Credit of Great Britain*. Mill said that it was the clearest exposition known to him in English of the subject with which it deals. I think, too, that I should have been rather more solemn about his work in Parliament, not only his efforts to abolish the slave trade, made in alliance with his cousin and close friend, William Wilberforce, but also his intelligent stand on the French Revolution, on Parliamentary Reform, and on Catholic Emancipation. "Cold, intellectual, public-spirited, fastidious, and full of integrity, Henry stands, and his hand rests upon a parliamentary bill"—it is thus that Mr. Forster describes Hoppner's striking portrait of Henry Thornton. I find rather more in the face and posture than that, more possibility of inner and intense experience than Mr. Forster is willing to admit; and I can't help feeling that in this sentence about a man of intelligence and integrity, whose mode of thought was political, the parliamentary bill ought not stand in the position of ironical anti-climax which it is made to occupy. But he is not my great-grandfather, and Mr. Forster must do as he pleases with his own.

Henry, who died at fifty, brought the Thorntons to their high point as a family, if only because he built Battersea Rise, the house that became the center of all the family emotion. Mr. Forster, as we know, is a great one for houses; and in this book he speaks of the Hertfordshire home of his boyhood and of its connection—wych-elm and all—with Howards End; we know too of his feeling for the lost Abinger. But Battersea Rise, although he saw it only once as a small boy and remembers it scarcely at all, is for him, by reason of the family adoration of it, the prototype of all consecrated houses. To the Thornton children, he says, "it was a perfect playground and in after years a sacred shrine."

It satisfied in them that longing for a particular place, a home, which is common amongst our upper and middle classes, and some of them transmitted that longing to their descendants, who have lived on into an age where it cannot be gratified. There will never be another Battersea Rise, and the modest imitations of it which lasted into the present century and became more and more difficult to staff have also disappeared.

Battersea Rise stood on Clapham Common. Clapham, of course, proposes the Clapham Sect; and it is rare indeed to come across a reference to this group which is not sniffishly superior. I recall the first mention of Clapham and its sect I ever heard—a professor of mine, a New York dandy of an older day, told us that Robert Browning's father had been a member of the Clapham Sect, and the dandiacal shrug of despair with which he imparted this information led me to see dull houses on a respectable street, and tea, and catarrh, and cotton gloves, and conversation rather more literate but not more enlightened than that of Mr. Stiggins of the Brick Lane Branch of the United Grand Junction Ebenezer Temperance Association (this is the elder Mr. Weller's Mr. Stiggins). And later, when I read Matthew Arnold's remarks about the British middle class, "drugged with business" and intoxicated by the religious emotions of Dissent, it was the Clapham Sectarians who came to my mind as examples, even though I knew that as Evangelicals they were not Dissenters.

Nothing, of course, could have been further from the truth. The life of the great Clapham families—the Wilberforces, the Macaulays, the Stephenses—was anything but dull and narrow. And Battersea Rise was nothing if not expansive. The recollection of it tells us how people once found it possible to think of themselves, how they could express their ideas of themselves in their manner of life—in, most especially, those great houses that, from century to century, from Jonson to Yeats, have captured the high fancy of the English poets. Henry Thornton was, to be sure, a wealthy man; but he was also a man of strict life, and he exemplified the quality that Mr. Forster says the Thorntons shared with two other nineteenth-century families, the Darwins and the Wedgwoods, the quality of remaining stubbornly "provincial and non-aristocratic." Battersea Rise was not an aristocrat's home, and Henry Thornton would not have wanted it to be; he was contemptuous of his brother Robert's social aspirations and much annoyed by the breakfast party which Robert gave for Queen Charlotte and her daughters, and he regretted that his father had allowed his sister to marry Lord Leven. But Henry Thornton's house represented an idea of dignity and freedom which, as Mr. Forster implies, scarcely anybody in England now would venture to express in a house, nor in America either.

The original house was a compact brick structure of the age of Queen Anne. When Henry Thornton bought it in 1792, Clapham, although only four or five miles from London, had but recently become safe, and the country was still unspoiled. The grounds were extensive and the gardens elaborate; and as late as 1887 cows were still maintained. Thornton threw out large wings on either side of the original house. "The heart of the house," says Mr. Forster, "was a fine oval library," which had been designed by Thornton's political chief, William Pitt. There were thirty-four bedrooms.

It was a house intended for a family, and the large family (nine children) flourished in it, and, of course, never got over it. In my father's house are many mansions: the nearest approach to heaven, the poets are always suggesting, is a really large and handsome house. They like to think of it as well run and very orderly. Battersea

Rise had, of course, its appropriate complement of gardens, pleas-ances, fruit trees, horses (ponies for the very young), and servants of crusty eccentricity and absolute permanence, mininstering angels of an inferior but self-respecting grade. The tone and the principles of the Thornton family were responsive to the best suggestions of their sacred house; among the principles was the hope and expectation of an actual heaven. The parents were good people. To be sure, they believed that they *should* be good, and this is an idea that alienates us from those who hold it and suggests to us that they have no true sensibility. But actually the Thorntons did have sensibility; they were not only good but kind and gracious, and not only to their friends but to their children and their servants. "Such was the atmo-sphere, such the household, into which Marianne Thornton was born: affections, comfort, piety, integrity, intelligence, public activity, private benevolence"—and Mr. Forster closes his list with what "transcend[ed] them all, an unshaken belief in a future life where the members of the household would meet again and would rec-ognize each other and be happy eternally."

Eventually Battersea Rise was but a pious memory to the children, and for some of them a bitter memory. The father died in 1815, the mother ten months later. This did not bring the life at Battersea Rise to an end; in the spacious manner of an older day, the young people who had been named as the children's guardians, Sir Robert and Lady Inglis, moved into the great house and the family lived on together. For two of the sisters, Isabella and Marianne, the life together survived the first marriage of the eldest brother, Henry, who had fallen heir to Battersea Rise; and Marianne lived on with Henry after Isabella's late marriage and Henry's widowerhood. But for Marianne the Battersea Rise life did not withstand the second mar-riage of Henry, for he chose as his second wife his Deceased Wife's Sister. It is hard for us now to understand the feelings that raged around the issue of whether or not a man should be allowed to marry the sister of his dead wife; by the Marriage Act of 1835, and on obscure doctrinal grounds, that inoffensive and often helpful relative had been placed within the prohibited degrees, and marriage with her carried not only canonical but also civil disabilities. The issue was felt by some to be one of morality, by others to be one of taste, by many to be one of loyalty to the church; and the liberals made it a political issue. The younger Henry Thornton fought for the passage of the parliamentary bill which would make his marriage legal, but the Deceased Wife's Sister Bill was not passed until 1907 and he had to go abroad to marry. The scandal itself was bad enough, but in addition this particular Deceased Wife's Sister was disliked; Emily Thornton was thought an inferior woman and a scheming one. Marianne removed to her own establishment and there was the inevitable family quarrel over furniture. She lived on Clapham Common, a half mile from Battersea Rise and within sound of its dinner bell, but her tie with the great house was at an end.

It was not until she was dying that she again opened communication with the house. The incident must be given in Mr. Forster's words. "A week before she died she wrote an extraordinary letter to Emily Thornton. She asked for some milk. No biographer could have foretold such a request, no novelist before Proust could have invented it. After thirty-five years' alienation she asks for some milk." The Deceased Wife's Sister, now a widow, replied graciously; milk from the cows of Battersea Rise was sent and letters of an affectionate sort were exchanged.

She was fifty-nine when she left Battersea Rise. There seems never to have been any question of her marrying. She was, Mr. Forster says, a good-looking girl; her letters speak of her intelligence, vivacity, and wit. But we have no record of any suitors—"not one hint of an affair, not the shadow of a name." And Mr. Forster speculates that she remained a spinster because she was in love with Battersea Rise, or because she was devoted to her brother Henry, or to her father's friend Wilberforce. (He was, by all present accounts of him, a most engaging man; it seems to have been his two sons who gave the name its unhappy aura, one of them, the Bishop of Oxford, being called, it is well known, Soapy Sam, the other, it is less

well known, Dull Robert.) Mr. Forster does not suggest that her
father was a possible barrier to matrimony. Yet Marianne's relation
to her father was exactly of the sort that often makes it difficult for
a girl to marry. Cold the elder Henry Thornton may have been, but
not to his eldest child. She was a timid little girl—phobic, as we
should now say—and he valued courage beyond any other quality;
yet she remembers long afterwards how he never laughed at her
fears or scolded her for them, but soothed and indulged her. He took
her very seriously; he wrote her charming and loving verses, and
he also taught her to examine her life and to mend it—Mr. Forster
finds him more attractive in the former activity than in the latter;
perhaps so, but certainly the two in conjunction must have been enor-
mously engaging to an intelligent child. He taught her to understand
public affairs and to discuss them with him; so that the devil would
not find employment for idle hands, he engaged her as "a sort of
secretary" as soon as she could write legibly. Add that he was a
handsome man, of perfect integrity, heroic in his notions of work,
and magnanimous in all his acts. It would have been hard for her
to look upon his like again.

She never sought to distinguish herself in the world. She had a
continuing active interest in the education of the lower classes,
derived from her old, close friend Hannah More, and she wrote
school readers which reflect the tart realism which was characteristic
of her. But she had no thought of making public use of her ready pen
and her powers of witty and robust observation. She did not even
seek her social life in the world of professional intellect; James
Knowles, who, as the founder of the Metaphysical Society and of
The Nineteenth Century, knew everybody worth knowing, was her
close friend, but she never entered his circle; the Macaulays were old
Claphamites, but the Tom who figures in her letters is a childhood
friend with whom she exchanges opinions and witticisms but never
Thomas Babington Macaulay, let alone Lord Macaulay. She did not
become literary, she became an aunt. She became the most impressive
aunt in history after Jane Austen. Of no other aunt except Jane

Austen—with whom she does indeed have certain literary affinities which she displays in her voluminous letters—could it have been said, as Mr. Forster says of Marianne Thornton, that a *cult* grew up around her. ". . . She never married and so she never altered. She represented continuity. . . . Childless herself, she became the family life that does not die with death."

Among her nephews and nieces she had a series of favorites; of these the last was Mr. Forster, to whom, in her devoted infatuation, she gave the nickname The Important One; by this dreadful appellation she undertook to arouse in Mr. Forster's young and early-widowed mother a due sense that her son must take priority over any plans she might have for her own life. There was a good deal of the Betsey Trotwood in her, and quite as much of the early Betsey Trotwood as of the later. She could be charmingly generous—and she could suffocate with attention, advice, and good sense. She really liked young people and knew how to please them, she had great tact in pleasing the young. But as she aged she pressed too hard, and interfered, and seemed insupportable. It is a common fate of the gifted and generous-minded old.

Mr. Forster calls his memoir of his great-aunt "a domestic biography," by which he would seem to suggest the homely modesty of his subject. But we must not be misled. The continuity that Marianne Thornton represented is indeed the "family life that does not die with death," but in this instance the family life stands for a good deal more than itself. It stands for a massive cultural tradition—the continuity of modern English culture is a family continuity.

In the first chapter of his biography of Leslie Stephen Mr. Noel Annan documented in considerable detail the English phenomenon that has often been noted in a general way, the extent to which the leading members of the intellectual professions are related to each other by ties of blood or marriage. A relatively few families of the upper middle class—some having a heritage of intellectual achievement that dates as far back as the seventeenth century, others coming to the intellectual life in the nineteenth century—proliferated, and intermarried, and continued in the intellectual life until now it may be said that the culture of England is in their hands. Mr. Annan has returned to this subject again and in even more detail in a fascinating essay called "The Intellectual Aristocracy" which he contributes to *Studies in Social History,* a collection prepared in tribute to G. M. Trevelyan, who, by his own family connection, handsomely illustrates Mr. Annan's point.

It is not possible here to suggest either the complexity or the stubborn consistency of the familial reticulation which has been in the making for several generations. Every learned profession—and some artistic professions, but the class established itself first in the universities and the emphasis is still largely on science and scholarship—is involved in it, is largely staffed by the descendants of the Macaulays, the Darwins, the Huxleys, the Arnolds, the Conybeares, and other families of similar kind. To an American, the phenomenon must inevitably seem faintly comic and entirely astonishing—for there have been very few American families that have established an intellectual line.

To some Americans the thought will inevitably occur that something more, or less, than intellect has been at work to make this "caucus of power or influence," as Mr. Annan calls it. But this is not the case. What we have, rather, is hereditary talent which takes pleasure in exercising itself and is encouraged by being given the opportunity to do so. Mr. Annan insists that it has not been unduly exclusive, that it is hospitable to properly qualified recruits. An Englishman and not an American must pass upon the accuracy of this judgment, just as an Englishman and not an American must look for the shortcomings of the class as a whole.

In the development of this class Evangelicism played an obvious part. Mr. Annan puts it thus: "There was the sense of dedication, of living with purpose, or working under the eye, if not of the great Taskmaster, of their own conscience—that organ which Evangelicism magnified so greatly. There was the sense of mission to improve the shining hour and the profession to which they had been called.

There was the sense of accounting for the talents with which Providence had endowed them. There was also the duty to hold themselves apart from a world given over to vanities which men of integrity rejected because they were content to labour in the vineyard where things of eternal significance grew—in the field of scholarship where results were solid not transient." To this Mr. Annan adds the influence of the pride of class, the sense at once of separateness from the aristocracy and of established individual worth, which is always a great help to an intellectual worker.

This, then, was the cultural-familial continuity that Marianne Thornton represented and that Mr. Forster tacitly celebrates in his "domestic biography."

1956

In Defense of Zola

O F THE great reputations of the nineteenth century perhaps none has suffered so much diminution as that of Zola. We all believe that we know all about Zola, whether we have read him or not—we know what he did, and what he stood for, whom he influenced and what his theory of the novel was, and what was wrong with it. But he has not for many years commanded our real interest, precisely, I suppose, because we believe we have him so thoroughly taped. Balzac is nowadays certainly not as important to us as he was when Henry James read us "The Lesson of Balzac," but Balzac is still considered and esteemed, if only because of his commanding patriarchal relation to the great line of the French novel which begins with him and ends with Proust. Stendhal and Flaubert are of course very firmly established with us. But of Zola we are no longer really aware. He exists for us chiefly as a fact in literary history. And if, in addition, we permit him to exist as—in Anatole France's famous funeral phrase—"a moment in the conscience of mankind," our literary refinement dictates that we temper our respect with a degree of condescension or indifference. He was valiant in the Dreyfus case, but can he speak to the secret places of our hearts? Except for a good essay by William Troy published ten or more years ago in *Partisan Review,* I can recall no instance of a contemporary American critic giving serious attention to this man whose work bulked so large in his own time and was so challenging in its bulk.

But Angus Wilson has written an excellent short book about Zola, an introductory study, as he calls it, which may do something to redress the balance in Zola's favor. Its defense of Zola's greatness as a literary artist is the more likely to be effective because of the high esteem in which Mr. Wilson is held as the author of notable short stories which, while they do indeed share Zola's exacerbated sense of the awfulness of man's life in society, are scarcely of a kind to make us expect from their author a ready sympathy with Zola's temperament and method.

Mr. Wilson begins his critical exposition with an account of the low condition of Zola's reputation, and his admiration for his author leads him, not unnaturally, to speak of the time as now ripe for a revival. I venture to disagree with him on the likelihood of such an event. Mr. Wilson is of the opinion that if the foreground of Zola's reputation were to be cleared of the debris that circumstance has deposited upon it, the enlightened reading public would have no reason for not being enthusiastically responsive to his manifest literary power. I am inclined to think that more than a policing operation is necessary to bring this about, that we shall have to make some basic revision of our contemporary taste before we can give Zola his full due. Yet the clearing away of the debris is certainly the required first step toward even the minimum of critical justice for Zola.

Like all writers who have had a wide and also a specific influence, Zola suffers from his disciples. As Mr. Wilson says, "To be largely responsible for George Moore and Arnold Bennett in England, Frank Norris and Dreiser in America, Heinrich Mann in Germany, Jules Romains in France, is an equivocal honor." The writers whom Mr. Wilson mentions are not lightly to be dismissed, at least not as lightly as Mr. Wilson does dismiss them. They are in a reputable and instructive and perhaps indispensable tradition. I have done my own worst by Dreiser and should be glad to do it again, but Dreiser is a man to be attacked, not waved away; and I should like to say a word for the novels of Arnold Bennett at a moment when a virtuous age has agreed to be horrified at Bennett's snobbery and philistinism. And yet of course Mr. Wilson is right in implying that most of the novelists in the naturalist tradition have come to seem dull and secondary to us and that they are likely to stand in the way of our knowing what the greatest of the naturalists can do in his own right.

Then Mr. Wilson cites as a barrier to our appreciation of Zola the "fourth-rate cultural superstructure" which Zola felt it necessary to erect upon his genius in order to provide a theoretical justification of its great productions. Mr. Wilson has chiefly in mind Zola's famous essay, "The Experimental Novel." Many great writers have ventured upon rationales of their own work, most of which have been not only true to the work itself but also great documents of criticism—the prefaces of Wordsworth, Victor Hugo, Arnold, Whitman, and Henry James are cases in point. But "The Experimental Novel," in which Zola undertook to establish the special validity of his fiction by showing that its methods were equivalent to those of the experimental physiologist, Claude Bernard, is not only a traduction of his genius but also a misrepresentation of his actual method. Balzac, who also liked to connect his work with medical science, had the good sense merely to suggest the connection and let the matter rest there; Zola argued the case, and the merest novice in literature can refute his argument. If we are to respond to Zola as he deserves, we must in good will forget his formulated theory.

Then we have to deal with the belief that Zola is a pornographic writer. In America Zola's works did not suffer the decisive repression which in England followed upon the prosecution and conviction and ruin of his English publishers, the Vizetellys. In England it was the courts, as well as some of the most advanced intellectual periodicals, that branded Zola a scabrous writer. In America it was the publishers themselves, many of whom issued his books only for their scandalous possibilities. In both countries the idea of Zola's salaciousness had an incidental and devastating effect upon the quality of the translations that were issued, most of them being fly-by-night and inaccurate, or much curtailed, almost all of them without elementary literary merit. The passage of time and the change of manners have of course vitiated the force of the charge of pornography, and nowadays it is presumed not to constitute a barrier between the enlightened reader and the writer against whom it is directed. Yet a generation that is not in the least uneasy with, say, Joyce's frankness about the biological functions, has been inclined to take a dim view of a similar frankness in Zola because it is conceived to be an element of the work of a writer who may be thought of as wholly without imagination, literal to the point of stupidity, even of brutality.

It is just here, on the ground of imagination, that Mr. Wilson makes his stand for Zola. He undertakes to demonstrate that the best of Zola's novels are so far from being literal and lacking in imagination that they may most truly be characterized by their poetic quality, by what Mr. Wilson calls their " 'black' poetry." This was the gist of the essay by Mr. Troy which I have mentioned, and it seems to me that any unprejudiced reader must come to agree with the two critics. The analogues with Zola's work are not to be found in science but in the work of such fantasts as Breughel and Bosch, or Ben Jonson, Baudelaire, and James Joyce—which is not surprising, for the line between a truly passionate naturalism and an extravagant fantasy is always a thin one. The obsessive contemplation of the objectivity of objects, the thingishness of things, is a step toward surrealism, perhaps toward madness.

Thus, to touch again upon Zola's reputation for pornography which has embarrassed and discouraged even enlightened readers, sex is for Zola never a thing to be observed with objectivity, let alone with pleasure: it is for him an outrageous moral-biological principle or force, appropriate to nature but not to human nature, the sign and means of the destruction of the human quality; Zola regards sex with a fascinated horror rather more extreme than Swift's. He understands it to be at once the mark and the agency of original sin, and its operation to make not only for brutality and corruption but for the grim macabre version of the comic which manifests itself when men cease to be human. Zola's view of sex may easily enough be said to be extravagant and distorted, but poetry does not always arise from balanced and objective views of things, and it is exactly Zola's obsessive view of sex that gives it in his work its moral and imaginative force, making it one of the chief agencies of that "'black' poetry" that Mr. Wilson so rightly insists on.

Sex is a pre-eminent element in most of Zola's novels, but it is omnipresent in *Restless House,* under which rather odd title *Pot-Bouille* has been translated and is now republished with an introduction by Mr. Wilson. The novel is one of the major engagements in the fierce war against the bourgeoisie to which virtually every French writer of genius of the nineteenth century gave the best of his energies. Zola mounts an attack in full force, undertaking to wipe out the enemy's base of spiritual supply. It is his intention to destroy the myth of bourgeois moral integrity by demonstrating the true nature of the vaunted family life of the middle class; he imputes to the people of militant respectability every sin and failure of sexuality that can suggest foolish passion, weakness of moral fibre, dullness of feeling, ruthlessness of conduct, lack of dignity—in sum, total depravity.

The book is a masterpiece. We begin it with a certain condescension, for the scheme of demonstration is not very promising: almost all the characters live in the same apartment house and it is here that most of the action takes place—how often we have been bored by the now familiar novelistic and dramaturgic device of the ant-colony or the beehive with a glass wall, how often we have failed to be surprised by what is supposed to be so surprising, the idea that in a hotel, a boarding-house, a Pullman car, a barracks, a ship, many people are doing various things, or the same thing, simultaneously! But, as often happens, the originator of the device uses it with a force and point not available to his imitators. In Zola's hands the organization of his story by means of a handy tight community is not the mechanical trick it becomes for his followers; it is organic and essential to his aesthetic effect, which is a very powerful one. It has the same function as the limitation of space in one of Breughel's satiric fantasies, which derive much of their dramatic force from the large number of persons who occupy the canvas—what wonders, by the way, Breughel might have done in illustration of the remark of one of Zola's characters, "France is one big bed"!—and it has the same function as Ben Jonson's claustral strictness of form in his comedies. Without it we should not have had the great and terrible scenes of the servant-maids in the offal-strewn courtyard, shouting their obscenities at each other, disclosing the secrets of every home, bitterly blowing the gaff on the respectability their labors make possible, often only just possible. Nor should we have had the rather dreadful but still very funny episode of Berthe Duveyrier running from door to door in her chemise as she flees from the wrath of a husband in whom righteous jealousy has at long last overcome neuralgia. Nor would we have the gem of ironic poetry in which, when the squalid passions have reached their climax and have sunk again to quiescence, the house resumes its gentle dream of its own order and respectability: "Behind the mahogany portals fresh founts of virtue played; . . . the maids sported aprons of dazzling whiteness, while, in the tepid silence of the staircase, all the pianos on all the floors flung out the self-same waltzes, making a music at once mystic and remote." Nothing could be finer than those waltzes.

We do not ask whether Zola's representation of the bourgeoisie is accurate or even if it is justified. We read his book for the pleasure of its fierce energy, for the strange pleasure we habitually derive from the indictment of the human kind. The work has a reality beyond anything that might be proved of the Parisian middle class of 1882, it has the reality of the author's rage and disgust with human inadequacy. The book, as I have said, has nothing to do with the scientific objectivity that Zola sought alliance with (except, perhaps, as the Kinsey Report has its own literary interest); it is in the great tradition of massive comic morality which I have tried to indicate by my mention of Breughel, Ben Jonson, and Swift, to whom we may add Hogarth, and, nearer at hand, Heine, the later Dickens, and Flaubert.

The adventures of its young protagonist, Octave Mournet, are of but subordinate interest in the novel. Octave has come from Marseilles to Paris to seek sexual adventure and his fortune—if possible, the latter through the former—and we are required to take note of his career because he is a member of the Mournet family, one of the three clans (the other two being the Rougons and the Macquarts) through which, in the great Rougon-Macquart series, Zola records the social and spiritual history of nineteenth-century France. He serves his turn as an example of the contemporary young man on the make, not without his decencies and sentimentalities but at bottom cowardly and crass. No doubt his career makes a useful sociological fact, but the greatness of the novel derives from the multitude of remorseless comic scenes with which he has essentially nothing to do: the chorus of amateurs at the Duveyriers' evening party performing the "Blessing of the Poniards" from *Les Huguenots;* their great climax out-topped by Berthe's cry from behind the window-draperies which makes it plain to all the company that she has succeeded in getting herself compromised by a man and now, according to the rules, must be married by him; Berthe and her family dancing savagely around the dining-room table to celebrate the capture of a fiancé after years of terrible effort and sacrifice, the candles they have lighted throwing their huge, wild shadows upon the wall; old M. Vabre's death-bed, his one regret being for the card-catalogue he has kept of *all* the pictures that have been hung in the Salon; the chaste, because cold, Clotilde Duveyrier perpetually practicing her piano scales, at the same time reading *La Revue de Deux Mondes* as, hour after hour, her fingers fly unregarded over the keyboard; the elaborate ritual of preparation and deceit which is required before the Campardon family can retire for the night—the wife, saved by a female complaint from all sexuality and responsibility, lying plump and rosy, creamed and coiffed, happily pillowed in the great conjugal bed, while the husband is doomed by his old passion for his wife's bony cousin to sleep fretfully in a bed not big enough for two, let alone for love; the retired government clerk

Vuillaume explaining to his daughter and her husband that if he, in the interests of economy and the good life, can sacrifice the pleasure of wearing the ribbon of his decoration so that he will not be put to the expense of buying a new one, the young people can see to it that they have no more babies. The moments of satiric comedy do not comprise the whole quality of the book—there is, for example of other things, a fine poetic charm and understanding in the representation of Marie Pichon, Vuillaume's daughter—but they are the chief element of its power.

With an admiration for Zola which is probably not less than Mr. Wilson's, I have yet discounted Mr. Wilson's prediction of a Zola revival. That is because it seems to me that Zola is, in a certain sense of the word, too *classic* an author to evoke the personal feelings which generally are engaged in a revival. In this respect Zola is very different from Stendhal and Flaubert, whom he so greatly admired. For all their devotion to the ideal of the work that shall be self-contained and complete in itself, Stendhal and Flaubert created personal legends which serve as the ambience in which we read their work and by which we gloss it. This is true to such an extent that the work often seems to have its importance less in itself than as a part of the personal legend. And the same thing may be said in greater or less degree of most of the great figures of modern literature. Yeats, Eliot, Lawrence, Joyce, Proust, Gide, Rilke, Kafka—all have their place in the modern pantheon not only as writers but as personalities, as notable cultural examples. Even the recent revival of respect for Dickens in some large part depends upon our new sense of him as a tragic personality. Zola permits no such secondary interest. Our concern with him ends with his work. His life provides us with no legend, or none beyond what the movies could exploit. He had, to be sure, no lack of the suffering and neurosis upon which modern legends are based. And certainly he was not remote from the problems of our culture—indeed, who more deeply implicated in them than he? But he was without the complexity, without the ambiguities and ambivalences which we most happily respond to, which we are inclined to believe are the only signs of authentic spiritual and artistic activity. If we are to experience Zola's genius, we must be content to take it all by itself as it appears in his work, without any bonus of the pleasure and self-esteem that may be drawn from an identification with the author's personality and travail. To me this seems a fair bargain, even a generous one; but not everyone will think so.

1953

A Ramble on Graves

ROBERT GRAVES has been very pleasantly in and out of our minds for some thirty-odd years. He was first known as one of the War Poets of the early Twenties, along with Siegfried Sassoon and Wilfred Owen; certain of the pieces of his first volumes were among the staples of the anthologies of the day and were as widely admired as they were Untermeyered. But then Mr. Graves distracted our attention from his early verse—a large part of which he soon repudiated—by the lively stir of his best-selling *Good-Bye to All That*, which is still one of the most interesting examples of the peculiarly English genre of the youthful autobiography. He has done admirable work as a critic of poetry, and very useful work as a defender of the liveliness, purity, and simplicity of the English language. He is unique as an historical novelist—he claims to have derived his historical method from his great-uncle, Leopold von Ranke—and around his Claudius novels there has formed a party of passionately loyal admirers, of which I count myself not exactly a card-carrying member but at least a fellow-traveler. It isn't impossible for Mr. Graves to produce a prose dud; such is his *Wife to Mr. Milton*, but the unhappy memory of this book was soon drowned in the pleasure of *Hercules My Shipmate*. I haven't read *King Jesus*, but those who have read it tell me that I should; if it has any of the cogent extravagance and tortured ingenuity in the manipulation of myth of *The White Goddess*, I shall be very glad indeed if I can find time to take their advice.

Nothing in his voluminous prose canon is calculated to make Mr. Graves a great, striking, exemplary figure in our literature. In all he has done in prose there is a happy intelligence at work, and a wide and curious scholarship, and gracefulness and verve. There is even seriousness, manifested in the intensity of his devotion to one past or another, in the consistency of his dislike for modern culture. But the seriousness has always been modified and mollified by a kind of conscious carelessness, or modesty, or irony. Nothing is easier than to perceive that Mr. Graves has been working in his own way with the matter of, say, Yeats and D. H. Lawrence; it is equally apparent that he has decided that his own way was the way of talent and not of genius.

This makes, I think, a very engaging spectacle. Mr. Graves as a prose writer is a first-rate secondary figure in our literature. Such figures are a British phenomenon—we don't breed them in America, and we don't know how to respond to them. An intelligent American who has a lively or a professional interest in literature wants only the Very Best, the *œuvre* that is certified by whatever literary Consumers' Union he subscribes to as having a top rating for spirituality, apocalypticality, and permanence. One might spend one's life pleasantly and very profitably with the secondary writers of the English nineteenth century, the writers whom no one would think to call "great," the odd, quirky spirits from George Borrow to Mark Rutherford, the travelers, the autobiographers, the essayists, the men who had a particular, perhaps eccentric, thing to say, and said it fully and well, with delight in what they were doing and no worry about greatness. And England is still able to produce and respond to these remarkable secondary figures. With us, however, the writer must be great or he is nothing; or believed to be great for a season, appropriately garlanded and anointed, and then sacrificed on the altar of our outraged literary conscience; then possibly "revived" again, only to be again interred—the American literary life makes a new chapter for *The Golden Bough*. And of course it is not only the readers and critics who support our savage demand for greatness, who insist that every writer carry a banner with the strange device, "Pike's Peak or Bust"; it is also the writers themselves.

There is much, then, to be said for Mr. Graves's election of the secondary role, and I should be glad to undertake to say all that I can. But the fact is that with the publication of his *Collected Poems* we have to see Mr. Graves in a new way—we have to see him as a poet of the first rank. The nature of his poetry repels the adjective "great." He cannot have, and does not try to have, the large dramatic appeal of Eliot or Yeats. It is of the nature of his achievement that he should not, for the modesty and the irony, the conscious, rather boyish, swagger that mark his work in prose are to be seen in his verse, where they are, however, transmuted into a positive element of a remarkable style.

It may be that for some readers there will be a certain difficulty in coming to terms with this style, with its preference for lightness as against weightiness (or, if you will, levity as against gravity), its conscious intention of vivacity and elegance. There would be less difficulty, perhaps none at all, if Mr. Graves were a painter rather than a poet. Painting is an art in which our crude passions for spiritual prestige—"Permit me to say that my tragic view of life is a great deal more tragic than your tragic view of life"—is far less in the ascendant than it is in literature. One has to be very young indeed to believe that the pleasure we take in Giotto or El Greco or Rembrandt is superior to, or at war with, the pleasure we take in Tiepolo or Canaletto or Guardi or Watteau. The autonomy of interest or charm of a painting is far more easily granted than is the autonomy of interest or charm of a poem. We are less inclined to feel that grace, elegance, lightness, or even apparent frivolity of theme, preclude the judgment of highest value. That is, I think, because in painting the elements of form, style, and technique speak to us more openly and eloquently than they do in poetry.

And that is why, I suppose, Mr. Graves has said that he writes poetry for poets only. In the Foreword to the thirty-one poems and nine "satires and grotesques" that make up the slim volume *Poems*

1938–1945, Mr. Graves said, ". . . I write poems for poets, and satires and grotesques for wits. For people in general I write prose, and am content that they should be unaware that I do anything else. To write poems for other than poets is wasteful." What Mr. Graves means is that, in our day, only poets can be counted on not to be misled by the lightness and clarity of his verse, by the irony and the humor; that only poets will be sufficiently aware of the tradition in which he writes, and of hearing the truth that lies not only in the doctrinal statements that the poem makes but in the justness of its diction, in the pitch and tone of its voice: they will know that the poem is a created thing, that it is a *creature,* and that it has its own creaturely life, and speaks in its own voice, which is to be judged as we judge the voice of an actual human creature, a person. When Mr. Graves says that he writes poems for poets, he is inviting us to consider with him the mystery of style and tone.

Probably there is no reasonable way of talking about the poet's tone, the quality of his voice, which may or may not be beautiful, but which must be truthful. Many things in poetry can be analyzed and argued about, but when it comes to the matter of the voice of the poet, there is nothing that the teacher or the critic can do except put the weight of whatever authority he has behind, or against, one or another way of speaking. Some years ago Randall Jarrell made a statement to the effect that no one could flatter himself that he had any feeling for poetry who did not know that Whitman's line "I am the man. I suffered. I was there" is of the very essence of poetry. Agreeing with Mr. Jarrell, I have often quoted his remark to students of literature, usually to be met with a blank stare of astonishment or the cagey understanding that I was perpetrating a perversity. No argument is possible. All that I can hope is that the tone of Whitman's line will begin to sound in the heads of those who do not in the least "understand" why it is supposed to be so good, and that it will eventually make the sound of other lines seem dull and vacant, or insincere, or affected. (The establishment of excellent lines in the memory is the best way of learning to respond properly to poetry;

with the exception of a few old-fashioned high-school teachers and
Mr. Auden and Mr. Barzun, I have never known anyone who shares
the passion of my belief in the value of memorizing poetry. A long
chapter in our cultural history could be written on the contemporary
belief that it is not only useless but cruel, mechanical, and repressive
to require young people to commit to memory a certain number of
passages from the great poems of the race—to, as the phrase used to
go, *get them by heart*.)

Here is an example of the voice in which Mr. Graves speaks:

> Children, if you dare to think
> Of the greatness, rareness, muchness,
> Fewness of this precious only
> Endless world in which you say
> You live, you think of things like this: . . .

It is thus that Mr. Graves begins "Warning to Children," which is a
complex and fairly difficult poem, and our pleasure is, or should be,
immediate. It is in part the pleasure of truth and belief: each word
is valued, but not overvalued; the rhetoric is just right, being the
rhetoric of literate colloquial speech, and our sense of the rhetoric,
of the easy management of the sentence, becomes conscious at the
end of the fourth line, where the enforced pause on "say" gives the
word a heavy emphasis and a double meaning (i.e., you say but you
don't really mean).

For me, the lines have the pleasure of an overtone of reminiscence.
The lift of the voice on the word "Children," hortatory and ad-
monitory, haunted me as something I had heard before, and my
memory, after a good deal of badgering, suddenly yielded the beginning of a poem by Robert Louis Stevenson in *A Child's Garden of
Verses,* unread for untold years:

> Children, you are very little,
> And your bones are very brittle;
> If you would grow great and stately,
> You must try to walk sedately.

> You must still be bright and quiet,
> And content with simple diet;
> And remain, through all bewildring,
> Innocent and honest children.

The poem, I find, is called "Good and Bad Children," and apart from the hortatory first word, there really isn't any particular similarity between it and Mr. Graves's poem; but it has a general affinity with certain aspects of Mr. Graves's verse, and certainly it would be characteristic of Mr. Graves to have had it in mind—if we speak of the tradition in which he writes, we may say he forms that tradition out of whatever is direct, immediate, and normal or habitual in utterance, and in this the verses of the nursery have, from the earliest days of Mr. Graves's writing, played a considerable part.

The mention of the tradition of the nursery makes it apposite to recall that Mr. Graves tells us in his autobiography that his perambulator was stopped and he was patted and kissed by Algernon Charles Swinburne, "an inveterate pram-stopper and patter and kisser." He goes on to recall that Swinburne, "when a very young man, went to Walter Savage Landor, then a very old man, and asked for and was given a poet's blessing." This explains a good deal—Landor's touch, without sufficient influence upon Swinburne, was transmitted to Graves. The Landor of the epigrams, of the lyrics, and of the short dramatic and narrative poems is very close to Graves. I don't know whether the college anthologies still talk of Landor's "classicism" and "Hellenism" with the effect of suggesting that he is somehow not an *English* poet—the fact is, of course, that he is pre-eminently English in his feeling for language. As with Mr. Graves, whatever he learned from the Greeks in the way of directness of statement serves to enforce, in his best work, his feeling for the genius of English. If we consider "When Helen first saw wrinkles in her face" and "The Death of Artemidora," and "Corinna to Tanagra, from Athens," and "Dirce" and "Mother, I cannot mind my wheel," and the ever-remembered "Rose Aylmer," we see how very close he is to Mr. Graves. That Landor should be in the pantheon of Mr. Graves's tradition, along with Skelton and Thomas Hardy, as well as with Herrick and Marvell, is not at all incongruous.

In 1916 D. H. Lawrence wrote a letter to Catherine Carswell in which he speaks in a very sour way about modern foreign literature and very sweetly about English literature, and what he says in this letter goes a long way toward defining the quality of Mr. Graves's poetry. "It amazes me," Lawrence wrote, "that we have bowed down and worshipped these foreigners as we have. Their art is so clumsy, really, and clayey, compared with our own. I read Deerslayer just before the Turgenev. And I can tell you what a come-down it was, from the pure and exquisite art of Fennimore [sic] Cooper—whom we count nobody—to the journalistic bludgeonings of Turgenev. They are all—Turgenev, Tolstoi, Dostoevsky, Maupassant, Flaubert —so very obvious and coarse, beside the lovely, mature and sensitive art of Fennimore Cooper or Hardy. It seems to me that our English art, at its best, is by far the sublest and loveliest and most perfect in the world. But it is characteristic of a highly developed nation to bow down to that which is more gross and raw and affected. . . . No, enough of this silly worship of foreigners. The most exquisite literature in the world is written in the English language."

This, I remind you, is Lawrence speaking, not Sir Arthur Quiller-Couch, or Sir Walter Raleigh, or some other English academic whom Dr. Leavis delights to slaughter. With our tendency to a solid Unesco attitude about cultures, which makes it morally wrong (undemocratic) to think of one culture as better than another, or even to think one's own culture more appealing than another, we will conclude that Lawrence is making nothing more than a crotchety parochial statement, even a chauvinistic statement. He is doing a great deal more than that. One of the things he is doing is implied by the epithet "exquisite"—"the most exquisite literature in the world is written in the English language." It is the language itself that is in question, and, of course, a particular aspect of the language, that aspect which Keats had in mind when, at the end of his struggle with Milton, he said, "English ought to be kept up." Admiring, even adoring Milton as he did, Keats yet repudiated this great master of his because Milton did not write English, and Keats wanted to cleave to English in its ordinariness, its immediacy, its "exquisiteness." This quality of English Mr. Graves himself has often discussed in his critical writings, and he everywhere exemplifies it in his poems, where the printed words always remind us that they are meant for the fate that so horrified Thoreau—they are meant to be spoken by a human mouth, equipped with tongue and teeth, hard and soft palate, and saliva:

> We looked, we loved, and therewith instantly
> Death became terrible to you and me.
> By love we disenthralled our natural terror
> From every comfortable philosopher
> Or tall, grey doctor of divinity:
> Death stood at last in his true rank and order.

Lawrence had in mind something more than language when he praised English literature with such petulant extravagance. He had in mind two parts of life that the English language seems especially well fitted to represent—the commonplace and nature. Lawrence's feeling for the commonplace (and he is, we remember, the genius who praised the high morality of the clean pocket-handkerchief and was a great scourer of pots) and for nature (and he is the great nature poet of our day) were made the more acute because he thought of the commonplace and nature as standing against the fierce modern intellectual will. Much the same thing can be said of Mr. Graves. The kitchen and the nursery and the drawing-room are recurrent in Mr. Graves's poems not because he is a poet of domesticity, nor because of some lingering piety of Victorianism, but because they stand for a certain kind of actuality which modulates the fierce modern intellectual will. They have the same purpose and effect as the modulation of Mr. Graves's language toward the actuality of speech. "Any honest housewife" is the title and the opening phrase of one of his poems—any honest housewife knows when the fish is fresh and the apples sound, and, in engaging domestic help, can "instantly distinguish from the workers/The lazy, the liars and the petty thieves."

> Does this denote a sixth peculiar sense
> Gifted to housewives for their vestal needs?

Or is it, the poem goes on to ask, "a failure of the usual five" in the critics and the intellectuals that they find it so very difficult to know what's what?

Of the china plate, cheaply bought and discovered to be a museum piece:

> Let it dispense sandwiches at a party
> And not be noticed in the drunken buzz,
> Or little cakes at afternoon tea
> When cakes are in demand.
>
> Let it regain a lost habit of life,
> Foreseeing death in honorable breakage
> Somewhere between the kitchen and the shelf—
> To be sincerely mourned.

The Lollocks of the poem of that name are horrible enough goblins, the more real and the more horribly splenetic because they are specifically English and specifically domestic.

> By sloth on sorrow fathered,
> These dusty-featured Lollocks
> Have their nativity in all disordered
> Backs of cupboard drawers.
>
> They play hide and seek
> Among collars and novels
> And empty medicine bottles,
> And letters from abroad
> That never will be answered.

The method of extermination:

> Sovereign against Lollocks
> Are hard broom and soft broom,

> To well comb the hair,
> To well brush the shoe,
> And to pay every debt
> So soon as it's due.*

Mr. Graves's transaction with nature may be thought of as being summed up in his poem "The Climate of Thought":

> The climate of thought has seldom been described.
> It is no terror of Caucasian frost,
> Nor yet that brooding Hindu heat
> For which a loin-rag and a dish of rice
> Suffice until the pestilent monsoon.
> But, without winter, blood would run too thin;
> Or, without summer, fires would burn too long.
> In thought the seasons run concurrently.

What follows is the prescription for an English landscape, sufficiently various, sufficiently charming, sufficiently strenuous. The poem is witty—and very serious: how serious it is can be brought to mind by recalling the New Mexico landscape that dominates the end of Lawrence's *St. Mawr,* which Lawrence describes with so fascinated a hatred, and all the other landscapes of modern literature, including that of Mars and the moon, which express our sense of mind being overwhelmed by brute matter. Mr. Graves has a passion for the old passions of the temperate zone—his impulse is all against being overwhelmed. He has a passion for pleasure, for love, for sexuality, for masculinity, for femininity, for activity, for rest; he has a passion for integrity of the self—and a passion for civilization. About his likes and dislikes, and sometimes about his way of putting them, there is much about him that suggests E. E. Cummings. The difference lies, I think, in their feeling for civilization. Graves is a less abstract writer than Cummings, as he is less lyrical; his pages are more *peopled* than Cummings's, more filled with actualities, because he accepts, as

---

* Keats used the recommended course against Lollocks: "Whenever I find myself growing vapourish, I rouse myself, wash and put on a clean shirt, brush my hair and clothes, tie my shoestrings neatly, and in fact adonize as I were going out—then all clean and comfortable I sit down to write."

Cummings does not, the idea of civilization. Cummings celebrates a way of feeling; Graves presupposes a way of life, and as a result there runs through his poems a vein of moralizing, very light and ironic, but persistent. He weights himself with common sense and with an ironic lore of the emotions. We can read him, as we could not read Cummings, as Cummings would not want to be read, side by side with Horace—not, of course, the Horace of academic convention, but the real Horace, the intense and passionate one. We can read him side by side with Montaigne. He is in the tradition of the men who, by the terms upon which they accept their ordinary humanity, make it extraordinary.

1955

The Morality of Inertia

A THEOLOGICAL seminary in New York planned a series
of lectures on "The Literary Presentations of Great Moral
Issues," and invited me to give one of the talks. Since I
have a weakness for the general subject, I was disposed to accept the
invitation. But I hesitated over the particular instance, for I was
asked to discuss the moral issues in *Ethan Frome*. I had not read
Edith Wharton's little novel in a good many years, and I remembered it with no pleasure or admiration. I recalled it as not at all the
sort of book that deserved to stand in a list which included *The
Brothers Karamazov* and *Billy Budd, Foretopman*. If it presented a
moral issue at all, I could not bring to mind what that issue was.
And so I postponed my acceptance of the invitation and made it
conditional upon my being able to come to terms with the subject
assigned to me.

Ethan Frome, when I read it again, turned out to be pretty much
as I had recalled it, not a great book or even a fine book, but a
factitious book, perhaps even a cruel book. I was puzzled to understand how it ever came to be put on the list, why anyone should
want to have it discussed as an example of moral perception. Then
I remembered its reputation, which, in America, is very considerable. It is sometimes spoken of as an American classic. It is often
assigned to high-school and college students as a text for study.

But the high and solemn repute in which it stands is, I am sure, in large part a mere accident of American culture. *Ethan Frome* appeared in 1911, at a time when, to a degree that we can now only wonder at, American literature was committed to optimism, cheerfulness, and gentility. What William Dean Howells called the "smiling aspects of life" had an importance in the literature of America some fifty years ago which is unmatched in the literature of any other time and place. It was inevitable that those who were critical of the prevailing culture and who wished to foster in America higher and more serious literature should put a heavy stress upon the grimmer aspects of life, that they would equate the smiling aspects with falsehood, the grimmer aspects with truth. For these devoted people, sickened as they were by cheerfulness and hope, the word "stark" seemed to carry the highest possible praise a critical review or a blurb could bestrow, with "relentless" and "inevitable" as its proper variants. *Ethan Frome* was admired because it was "stark"— its action, we note, takes place in the New England village of Starkville—and because the fate it describes is *relentless* and *inevitable*.

No one would wish to question any high valuation that may be given to the literary representation of unhappy events—except, perhaps, as the high valuation may be a mere cliché of an intellectual class, except as it is supposed to seem the hallmark of the superior sensibility and intelligence of that class. When it is only this, we have the right, and the duty, to look sniffishly at starkness, and relentlessness, and inevitability, to cock a skeptical eye at grimness. And I am quite unable to overcome my belief that *Ethan Frome* enjoys its high reputation because it still satisfies our modern snobbishness about tragedy and pain.

We can never speak of Edith Wharton without some degree of respect. She brought to her novels a strong if limited intelligence, notable powers of observation, and a genuine desire to tell the truth, a desire which in some part she satisfied. But she was a woman in whom we cannot fail to see a limitation of heart, and this limitation makes itself manifest as a literary and moral deficiency of her work, and of *Ethan Frome* especially. It appears in the deadness of her prose, and more flagrantly in the suffering of her characters. Whenever the characters of a story suffer, they do so at the behest of their author—the author is responsible for their suffering and must justify his cruelty by the seriousness of his moral intention. The author of *Ethan Frome,* it seemed to me as I read the book again to test my memory of it, could not lay claim to any such justification. Her intention in writing the story was not adequate to the dreadful fate she contrived for her characters. She indulges herself by what she contrives—she is, as the phrase goes, "merely literary." This is not to say that the merely literary intention does not make its very considerable effects. There is in *Ethan Frome* an image of life-in-death, of hell-on-earth, which is not easily forgotten: the crippled Ethan, and Zeena, his dreadful wife, and Matty, the once charming girl he had loved, now bedridden and querulous with pain, all living out their death in the kitchen of the desolate Frome farm—a perpetuity of suffering memorializes a moment of passion. It is terrible to contemplate, it is unforgettable, but the mind can do nothing with it, can only endure it.

My new reading of the book, then, did not lead me to suppose that it justified its reputation, but only confirmed my recollection that *Ethan Frome* was a dead book, the product of mere will, of the cold hard literary will. What is more, it seemed to me quite unavailable for any moral discourse. In the context of morality, there is nothing to say about *Ethan Frome*. It presents no moral issue at all.

For consider the story it tells. A young man of good and gentle character is the only son of a New England farm couple. He has some intellectual gifts and some desire to know the world, and for a year he is happy attending a technical school. But his father is incapacitated by a farm accident, and Ethan dutifully returns to manage the failing farm and sawmill. His father dies; his mother loses her mental faculties, and during her last illness she is nursed by a female relative whom young Ethan marries, for no other reason than that he is bemused by loneliness. The new wife, Zeena, immediately becomes a shrew, a harridan and a valetudinarian—she lives only to be ill. Because Zeena now must spare herself, the Fromes take into their home a gentle and charming young girl, a destitute cousin of the wife. Ethan and Matty fall in love, innocently but deeply. The wife, perceiving this, plans to send the girl away, her place to be taken by a servant whose wages the husband cannot possibly afford. In despair at the thought of separation Matty and Ethan attempt suicide. They mean to die by sledding down a steep hill and crashing into a great elm at the bottom. Their plan fails: both survive the crash, Ethan to be sorely crippled, Matty to be bedridden in perpetual pain. Now the wife Zeena surrenders her claim to a mysterious pathology and becomes the devoted nurse and jailer of the lovers. The terrible tableau to which I have referred is ready for inspection.

It seemed to me that it was quite impossible to talk about this story. This is not to say that the story is without interest as a story, but what interest it may have does not yield discourse, or at least not moral discourse.

But as I began to explain to the lecture committee why I could not accept the invitation to lecture about the book, it suddenly came over me how very strange a phenomenon the book made—how remarkable it was that a story should place before us the dreadful image of three ruined and tortured lives, showing how their ruin came about, and yet propose no moral issue of any kind. And if *issue* seems to imply something more precisely formulated than we have a right to demand of a story, then it seemed to me no less remarkable that the book had scarcely any moral reverberation, that strange and often beautiful sound we seem to hear generated in the air by a tale of suffering, a sound which is not always music, which does not always have a "meaning," but which yet entrances us, like the random notes of an Aeolian harp, or merely the sound of the wind in the chimney. The moral sound that *Ethan Frome* makes is a dull thud. And this seemed to me so remarkable, indeed, that in the very act of saying why I could not possibly discuss *Ethan Frome,* I found the reason why it must be discussed.

It is, as I have suggested, a very great fault in *Ethan Frome* that it presents no moral issue, sets off no moral reverberation. A certain propriety controls the literary representation of human suffering. This propriety dictates that the representation of pain may not be, as it were, gratuitous; it must not be an end in itself. The naked act of representing, or contemplating, human suffering is a self-indulgence, and it may be a cruelty. Between a tragedy and a spectacle in the Roman circus there is at least this much similarity, that the pleasure both afford derives from observing the pain of others. A tragedy is always on the verge of cruelty. What saves it from the actuality of cruelty is that it has an intention beyond itself. This intention may be so simple a one as that of getting us to do something practical about the cause of the suffering or to help actual sufferers, or at least to feel that we should; or it may lead us to look beyond apparent causes to those which the author wishes us to think of as more real, such as Fate, or the will of the gods, or the will of God; or it may challenge our fortitude or intelligence or piety.

A sense of the necessity of some such intention animates all considerations of the strange paradox of tragedy. Aristotle is concerned to solve the riddle of how the contemplation of human suffering can possibly be pleasurable, of why its pleasure is permissible. He wanted to know what literary conditions were needed to keep a tragedy from being a display of horror. Here it is well to remember that the Greeks were not so concerned as we have been led to believe to keep all dreadful things off the stage—in the presentation of Aristotle's favorite tragedy, the audience saw Jocasta hanging from a beam, it saw the representation of Oedipus's bloody eyesockets. And so Aristotle discovered, or pretended to discover, that tragedy did certain things to protect itself from being merely cruel. It chose, Aristotle said, a certain kind of hero; he was of a certain social and moral stature; he had a certain degree of possibility of free choice; he must justify his fate, or seem to justify it, by his moral condition, being neither wholly good nor wholly bad, having a particular fault that collaborates with destiny to bring about his ruin. The purpose of all these specifications for the tragic hero is to assure us that we observe something more than mere passivity when we witness the hero's suffering, that the suffering has, as we say, some meaning, some show of rationality.

Aristotle's theory of tragedy has had its way with the world to an extent which is perhaps out of proportion to its comprehensiveness and accuracy. Its success is largely due to its having dealt so openly with the paradox of tragedy. It serves to explain away any guilty feelings that we may have at deriving pleasure from suffering.

But at the same time that the world has accepted Aristotle's theory of tragedy, it has also been a little uneasy about some of its implications. The element of the theory that causes uneasiness in modern times is the matter of the stature of the hero. To a society based in egalitarian sentiments, the requirement that the hero be a man of rank seems to deny the presumed dignity of tragedy to men of lesser status. And to a culture which questions the freedom of the will, Aristotle's hero seems to be a little beside the point. Aristotle's prescription for the tragic hero is clearly connected with his definition, in his *Ethics,* of the nature of an ethical action. He tells us that a truly ethical action must be a free choice between two alternatives. This definition is then wonderfully complicated by a further requirement—that the moral man must be so trained in making the right choice that he makes it as a matter of habit, makes it, as it were, instinctively. Yet it *is* a choice, and reason plays a part in its making. But we, of course, don't give to reason the same place in the moral life that Aristotle gave it. And in general, over the last hundred and fifty years, dramatists and novelists have tried their hand at the representation of human suffering without the particular safeguards against cruelty which Aristotle perceived, or contrived. A very large part of the literature of Western Europe may be understood in terms of an attempt to invert or criticize the heroic prescription of the hero, by burlesque and comedy, or by the insistence on the commonplace, the lowering of the hero's social status and the diminution of his power of reasoned choice. The work of Fielding may serve as an example of how the mind of Europe has been haunted by the great image of classical tragedy, and how it has tried to lay that famous ghost. When Fielding calls his hero Tom Jones, he means that his young man is not Orestes or Achilles; when he calls him a foundling, he is suggesting that Tom Jones is not, all appearances to the contrary notwithstanding, Oedipus.

Edith Wharton was following where others led. Her impulse in conceiving the story of Ethan Frome was not, however, that of moral experimentation. It was, as I have said, a purely literary impulse, in the bad sense of the word "literary." Her aim is not that of Words-worth in any of his stories of the suffering poor, to require of us that we open our minds to a realization of the kinds of people whom suffering touches. Nor is it that of Flaubert in *Madame Bovary,* to wring from solid circumstances all the pity and terror of an ancient tragic fable. Nor is it that of Dickens or Zola, to shake us with the perception of social injustice, to instruct us in the true nature of social life and to dispose us to indignant opinion and action. These are not essentially literary intentions; they are moral intentions. But all that Edith Wharton has in mind is to achieve that grim tableau of which I have spoken, of pain and imprisonment, of life-in-death. About the events that lead up to this tableau, there is nothing she finds to say, nothing whatever. The best we can conclude of the meaning of her story is that it might perhaps be a subject of discourse in the context of rural sociology—it might be understood to exemplify the thesis that love and joy do not flourish on poverty-stricken New England farms. If we try to bring it into the context of morality, its meaning goes no further than certain cultural considerations—that is, to people who like their literature to show the "smiling aspects of life," it may be thought to say, "This is the aspect that life really has, as grim as this"; while to people who repudiate a literature that repre-sents only the smiling aspects of life it says, "How intelligent and how brave you are to be able to understand that life is as grim as this." It is really not very much to say.

And yet there is in *Ethan Frome* an idea of considerable importance. It is there by reason of the author's deficiencies, not by reason of her powers—because it suits Edith Wharton's rather dull intention to be content with telling a story about people who do not make moral decisions, whose fate cannot have moral reverberations. The idea is this: that moral inertia, the *not* making of moral decisions, constitutes a large part of the moral life of humanity.

This isn't an idea that literature likes to deal with. Literature is charmed by energy and dislikes inertia. It characteristically represents morality as positive action. The same is true of the moral philosophy of the West—has been true ever since Aristotle defined a truly moral act by its energy of reason, of choice. A later development of this tendency said that an act was really moral only if it went against the inclination of the person performing the act: the idea was parodied as saying that one could not possibly act morally to one's friends, only to one's enemies.

Yet the dull daily world sees something below this delightful preoccupation of literature and moral philosophy. It is aware of the morality of inertia, and of its function as a social base, as a social cement. It knows that duties are done for no other reason than that they are said to be duties; for no other reason, sometimes, than that the doer has not really been able to conceive of any other course, has, perhaps, been afraid to think of any other course. Hobbes said of the Capitol geese that saved Rome by their cackling that they were the salvation of the city, not because they were they but there. How often the moral act is performed not because we are we but because we are there! This is the morality of habit, or the morality of biology. This is Ethan Frome's morality, simple, unquestioning, passive, even masochistic. His duties as a son are discharged because he is a son; his duties as a husband are discharged because he is a husband. He does nothing by moral election. At one point in his story he is brought to moral crisis—he must choose between his habituated duty to his wife and his duty and inclination to the girl he loves. It is quite impossible for him to deal with the dilemma in the high way that literature and moral philosophy prescribe, by reason and choice.

Choice is incompatible with his idea of his existence; he can only elect to die.

Literature, of course, is not wholly indifferent to what I have called the morality of habit and biology, the morality of inertia. But literature, when it deals with this morality, is tempted to qualify its dullness by endowing it with a certain high grace. There is never any real moral choice for the Félicité of Flaubert's story "A Simple Heart." She is all pious habit of virtue, and of blind, unthinking, unquestioning love. There are, of course, actually such people as Félicité, simple, good, loving—quite stupid in their love, not choosing where to bestow it. We meet such people frequently in literature, in the pages of Balzac, Dickens, Dostoievski, Joyce, Faulkner, Hemingway. They are of a quite different order of being from those who try the world with their passion and their reason; they are by way of being saints, of the less complicated kind. They do not really exemplify what I mean by the morality of inertia. Literature is uncomfortable in the representation of the morality of inertia or of biology, and overcomes its discomfort by representing it with the added grace of that extravagance which we denominate saintliness.

But the morality of inertia is to be found in very precise exemplification in one of Wordsworth's poems. Wordsworth is preeminent among the writers who experimented in the representation of new kinds and bases of moral action—he has a genius for imputing moral existence to people who, according to the classical morality, should have no moral life at all. And he has the courage to make this imputation without at the same time imputing the special grace and interest of saintliness. The poem I have in mind is ostensibly about a flower, but the transition from the symbol to the human fact is clearly, if awkwardly, made. The flower is a small celandine, and the poet observes that it has not, in the natural way of flowers, folded itself against rough weather:

> But lately, one rough day, this Flower I passed
> And recognized it, though in altered form,

Now standing as an offering to the blast,
And buffeted at will by rain and storm.

I stopped, and said with inly-muttered voice,
It doth not love the shower nor seek the cold;
This neither is its courage nor its choice,
But its necessity in being old.

Neither courage nor choice, but necessity: it cannot do otherwise. Yet it acts as if by courage and choice. This is the morality imposed by brute circumstance, by biology, by habit, by the unspoken social demand which we have not the strength to refuse, or, often, to imagine refusing. People are scarcely ever praised for living according to this morality—we do not suppose it to be a morality at all until we see it being broken.

This is morality as it is conceived by the great mass of people in the world. And with this conception of morality goes the almost entire negation of any connection between morality and destiny. A superstitious belief in retribution may play its part in the thought of simple people, but essentially they think of catastrophes as fortuitous, without explanation, without reason. They live in the moral universe of the Book of Job. In complex lives, morality does in some part determine destiny; in most lives it does not. Between the moral life of Ethan and Matty and their terrible fate we cannot make any reasonable connection. Only a moral judgment cruel to the point of insanity could speak of it as anything but accidental.

I have not spoken of the morality of inertia in order to praise it but only to recognize it, to suggest that when we keep our minds fixed on what the great invigorating books tell us about the moral life, we obscure the large bulking dull mass of moral fact. Morality is not only the high, torturing dilemmas of Ivan Karamazov and Captain Vere. It is also the deeds performed without thought, without choice, perhaps even without love, as Zeena Frome ministers to Ethan and Matty. The morality of inertia, of the dull, unthinking round of duties, may, and often does, yield the immorality of inertia; the example that will most readily occur to us is that of the good simple people, so true to their family responsibilities, who gave no thought to the concentration camps in whose shadow they lived. No: the morality of inertia is not be praised, but it must be recognized. And Edith Wharton's little novel must be recognized for bringing to our attention what we, and literature, so easily forget.

1955

The Dickens of Our Day

NO ONE, I think, is any longer under any illusion about Dickens. It is now clear that he is one of the two greatest novelists of England, Jane Austen being the other. His faults and failures as a writer are no longer to be discovered, which is not to say they do not exist but only that they are by now well known and don't seem to matter—we understand them to be the small price we pay to a past culture for the amazing personal genius which time in its passage seems only to make the more transcendent.

Some fifty years ago, G. K. Chesterton, a far greater critic than his present reputation might suggest, was under the necessity, when he wrote about Dickens, of championing him against the advanced aesthetic opinion of the day. Chesterton's strategy was to say that Dickens was perhaps not a novelist at all, only a tremendous genius working in some indeterminate genre. He was put to this shift because the opinion with which he was contending held a theory of the novel that made it out to be the dutiful child of science and classicism, having a certain kind of verisimilitude (and no other) and a certain kind of form. I can attest to the necessity of Chesterton's maneuver, for I was present at, as it were, the beginning of the end of the highbrow resistance to Dickens—I remember with what a smile of saying something daring and inacceptable John Erskine told an undergraduate class that some day we would understand that plot and melodrama were good things for a novel to have and that *Bleak House* was a very good novel indeed. I took this to be at best a lively paradox of Erskine's, intended to shock his young listeners, at worst an aberration of his critical intellect. And when a classmate, Clifton Fadiman, ventured even beyond Erskine's audacity and, having submitted his mind to Chesterton, went about among his friends saying that Dickens, not merely in this novel or that, but in his totality, was a very great writer indeed, I was convinced that this was mere affectation on Fadiman's part. I had been, as people used to say, brought up on Dickens, or at least I had been brought up on the myth of being brought up on Dickens, and there seemed to me no possibility that so familial a figure could have any true virtue for an intelligent and advanced person, such as I believed Erskine and Fadiman to be, such as I hoped to be myself.

But the literary sophistication of one day is the literary obscurantism of the next. We have come to accept, and even to demand, degrees of intensity and distortion which, to refined minds, once seemed inadmissible. Our own advanced tastes have taught us how to read the work of Dickens that was naturally and easily accessible to the simplest reader of a hundred years ago. What Dostoievski learned from Dickens has revealed to us what Dickens had to teach. The young Henry James denounced _Our Mutual Friend_ for Mrs. Wilfer's gloves and the psychological impossibilities of the story—it was necessary for him to reject what he thought to be Dickens's extravagances in order to make room for his own; but James's extravagances have in turn helped us in our acceptance of Dickens's. Indeed, there is scarcely a cherished modern text that does not instruct us in this way—we cannot read Kafka or Lawrence or Faulkner without learning a little better how to read Dickens.

I can offer what I think is an interesting example of this process. Mr. Edgar Johnson, of whose remarkable new biography of Dickens I shall speak in a moment, in the course of his critical discussion of _Our Mutual Friend_ ventures on a comparison of this novel with _The Waste Land_. I have lately been reading Dickens with a class of mine, and I put the comparison to the students, asking them whether they thought it legitimate or perhaps far-fetched. A considerable

number of students of course knew Eliot's poem. So far from thinking the comparison far-fetched, they celebrated its legitimacy by
sending up a pyrotechnic display of analogies to be drawn between
the two works, remarking that they had in common the great op-
pressive images of London, and the dominating symbols of waste
and decay, and the extreme representations of boredom and *taedium
vitae,* and the scenes in lower-class bars, and the River Thames that
cannot wash the city clean but becomes itself soiled and foul, and the
deaths by water and the hope of rebirth, and the drowned sailors,
and the bridges and the omnipresent financial transactions; and one
student said that, as to the lost consignment of figs in *The Waste
Land,* it was worthy of note that Mr. Podsnap was in the Marine
Insurance business.

I have suggested that Dickens's place in the culture of the family
was what used to stand in the way of his acceptance by the readers
of a generation or two ago—there had come a time when the set of
Dickens's works was a sort of surrogate for the family hearth itself,
and it was only natural that it should be thought of rather vindic-
tively when the young men detached themselves from their homes.
And Dickens was domestic too in the sense that so much of his reference was to hearth and home, to familial connections, which he was
thought to glorify and sentimentalize. In point of fact, of course,
most of Dickens's representations of home life are terribly bitter—
he specializes in the depiction of inadequate parents and no one knew
better than he how truly the Victorian family could be, what another
Victorian writer called it, a hell. But at the same time it is true that
Dickens does love to represent the fulfillment of all natural spon-
taneous emotions in the family. To the advanced and sensitive
readers of even a decade or two ago, this seemed a wrong thing to
do, or at least an irrelevant and old-fashioned thing to do. The self
and the family were declared to be incompatible and it was the self
that the advanced and sensitive reader was concerned with. Yet—and
this constitutes a really notable fact in the history of our culture—if
we now look back over the great literary enterprises of our time, we

cannot but be struck by how deeply preoccupied these are with the family idea. Granting their emphasis upon alienation, the power of their images of alienation derives from the sense of the violation of their childhood peace and familial security. Kafka, to take but one example, would seem to be a temperament as far removed as possible from Dickens; yet to read Kafka's life and works under the aspect of the parental relations of, say, *Dombey and Son,* of *David Copperfield* and of *Little Dorrit* (this last especially pertinent with its overshadowing prisons and its Circumlocution Office in which no official may ever give an answer) is to understand the perfect continuity of the twentieth century with the nineteenth. And Lawrence, Proust, Joyce, Faulkner give to the family a place in their vision of life which is no less fundamental than that of Dickens. It is much to the point that of recent years it has become almost fashionable to compare Dickens with Blake, who holds so notable a place in our modern pantheon as the first enunciator of the great modern theme of the "little boy lost," of the child's elemental emotions and familial trust being violated by the ideas and institutions of modern life.

In short, our contemporary literature has had the effect of bringing to light, of developing as on a photographic film, our sense of the importance and profundity and accuracy of Dickens. In that last difficult matter of accuracy, events have played their part in settling the question in Dickens's favor. We who have seen Hitler, Goering, and Goebbels put on the stage of history, and Pecksniffery institutionalized in the Kremlin, are in no position to suppose that Dickens ever exaggerated in the least the extravagance of madness, absurdity, and malevolence in the world—or, conversely, when we consider the resistance to these qualities, the amount of goodness. "When people say Dickens exaggerates, it seems to me that they can have no eyes and ears. They probably have only *notions* of what things and people are"—thus, in justified irritation, Santayana: and who now, with the smallest experience of life, would fail to agree with him?

Nothing, then, stands in the way of our response to Dickens as an artist, and as our admiration becomes more and more confirmed, it is inevitable that our interest in Dickens the man should be established with it. Not that at any time there has been a lack of interest in the man. There could scarcely be, the man being what he was, the effect of his work on the world being what it was. Nor, indeed, has there ever been any difficulty about indulging our curiosity. Dickens's character is so large and well defined that it cannot be obscured even by an unsatisfactory biography, and on the whole Dickens has not been too badly served by those who have written about his life. But not until Edgar Johnson's *Charles Dickens: His Tragedy and Triumph* have we had the story as it ought to be told.

The first virtue of Mr. Johnson's biography is its size. Men who have lived in a large way must be written about on a commensurate scale, and men who truly engage our interest and affection do so in detail. The incidents of childhood cannot be too many, the process of growth cannot be too precisely described, the data of business transactions and domestic arrangements cannot be overabundant—where our heart is, every fact is of importance, every fact speaks to us. It is impossible not to feel this about Dickens's life, which does not mean that we are on our way to joining the company of the genial madmen who belong to Dickens Fellowships and make Dickens Tours and, on a higher stage of development, write learned notes for *The Dickensian*. The mere desire for a true knowledge of Dickens's life requires detail, every possible detail—it is a life that cannot be understood in its essence unless it is seen in all its plethora of existence.

Thus, it is only with all the details before us that we recognize that Dickens's life had in it an element of the miraculous. I intend the word almost literally, and refer to Dickens's ability to manipulate time, to make the sun stand still. Obviously, all the Victorians stood in a different relation to time than we do, either because time was different in their time, or because, more likely, their personalities were different from ours. They did not feel about that job in the Post Office, or the Education Office, or India House that it was more important and powerful than they were, and this meant that they thought a shelf was something on which to put not themselves but their books, which they wrote as they could in those odd hours that they knew how to make infinitely expansible. But of all the Victorians Dickens was surely the greatest chronological prestidigitator. One has only to look at the volume of Dickens letters which Mr. Johnson recently edited in his careful and enlightening way (it is called, unfortunately, *The Heart of Dickens*) to see that Dickens had no ordinary mortal's relation to time. These are the letters to his friend, the great heiress, Lady Burdett Coutts, whom Dickens advised and aided in her charitable enterprises. When it came to good works, there was for Dickens no sitting in Committee and agreeing that the Chairman should instruct the Director to tell his staff to do this or that. If a loft had to be found for a Ragged School, Dickens found it and bargained with the landlord; if a home was to be established to rehabilitate prostitutes, Dickens found the house, furnished and arranged it, engaged the matrons and discharged them, laid down the principles and rules, and dealt with the difficult disciplinary problems. Meanwhile, it being known that Dickens was a benevolent man, everybody who was in trouble, or whose friend was in trouble, applied to him, and he saw them and responded to their needs. And all the arrangements that were made, and all the new miseries that were brought to his attention, had to be reported to Lady Coutts, not only by personal calls but in letters. Those letters that Dickens wrote in his lifetime! To Lady Coutts alone there are over five hundred; the great three-volume Nonesuch Edition runs to twenty-five hundred pages and over a million words, and Mr. Johnson tells us that "even the published letters are perhaps not half of those Dickens wrote"—to his friends, to his family, to his publishers, to his employees, to people he never heard of, almost every one of them a true communication, touched with some real element of his personality, so that in their aggregate they make up as full a record of his life as any human being ever accumulated, and would seem to us to be in themselves a life work.

The supervision of the Coutts benevolences were of course but a small part of Dickens's public activity. His sense of solidarity with the brothers of his craft was very strong, and this perpetually involved him in funds and guilds, which made it happily necessary for him to plan those great benefit performances of his, amateur theatricals which he insisted should be produced with more than professional care, and which he therefore—*therefore:* for he was sure that when a thing was to be properly done, he himself must do it—oversaw to the last button, and directed, and acted in, performing with such power and passion that many spoke of him as the greatest actor of his time. Then he was a great editor, and not merely a conceiving or directing editor, although he was that, but also a working editor who extensively revised and rewrote the copy that passed through his hands. His family was large—his parents were always a charge and a trial; two of his brothers were venal nuisances; his sister died after a long, pathetic illness; all claimed Dickens's attention and his purse. His many children occupied him intensely; their nursery plays at Christmas took nearly as much doing as one of his great public amateur productions, and their schooling and careers were closely supervised. He was called upon by everyone for everything, and not least for friendship, which he loved to give, for he had a kind of genius for it. The mere record of his conviviality is exhausting—it was a more generously social age than ours, and Dickens was always giving or being given dinners, large or small, to celebrate something, his going to America or his coming home or the completion of a book; when he had finished *The Chimes* in Italy nothing would do but that he rush madly home to read it to a group of his friends and reduce them to tears and then dash back to Italy again.

It is also true that he wrote novels. And perhaps no other man could have endured, as Dickens did, going out to buy a quire of paper for the next number of *Copperfield,* and at the stationer's overhearing a lady asking for the new installment of *Copperfield*— no, not the one the shop-keeper offered her, she had read that; she wanted the *new* one: the one that, as Dickens realized, was yet to be begun on the paper he was just buying.

For Mr. Johnson's scholarship there could be no higher praise than to say it is equal to the job it undertook. And by his scholarship I do not mean merely his pertinacity in accumulating the facts, but his modesty in submitting himself to them, his justness in sorting out their proportionate values. Nowhere does he impose himself—he is the servant of fact, and the fact, as is its nature, reciprocates handsomely and gives him one of the most fascinating and moving of stories. This firm objectivity of the biographer is apparent even in the chapters in which he deals critically with the novels. Mr. Johnson was well advised to give as much space to criticism as he does; without this close consideration of the novels, the account of Dickens's life would have lost a dimension. And in what he says of the novels Mr. Johnson is always central and always illuminating, both by reason of his critical observation and by reason of his adduction of social fact. As an example of the latter, it will, I think, mean as much to other admirers of *Our Mutual Friend* as it meant to me to have it clearly explained just what the composition of a London dust-heap was and just what its value might be (as much as £40,000!), for without this information we are likely to think of the whole garbage-symbolism of the book as striking but a little factitious. But indeed, on the score of social history, I know of no single book which tells us so much as Mr. Johnson's about the nature of Victorian life, both great matters and small.

We cannot say less of Mr. Johnson's book than that it is the definitive life of Dickens. And to say this is to say that it is a splendid achievement and a work of superlative interest and charm.

1952

Edmund Wilson:
A Backward Glance

I N 1929 I signalized my solidarity with the intellectual life by taking an apartment in Greenwich Village. I was under no illusion that the Village was any longer in its great days—I knew that in the matter of residential preference I was a mere epigone. So much so, indeed, that my apartment was not in a brownstone house or in a more-or-less reconditioned tenement, but in a brand-new, yellow-brick, jerry-built, six-story apartment building, exactly like the apartment buildings that were going up all over the Bronx and Brooklyn. Still, the Village was the Village, there seemed no other place in New York where a right-thinking person might live, and many of my friends held the same opinion and were settled nearby. What is more, my address was Bank Street, which, of all the famous streets of the Village, seemed to me at the time to have had the most distinguished literary past, although I cannot now remember my reasons for thinking so. And to validate its present dignity, to suggest that what the Village stood for in American life was not wholly a matter of history, Edmund Wilson lived just across the way. Someone had pointed out his apartment to me and I used to take note of his evening hours at his desk.

I did not meet Wilson until later in the year, when I called on him at the offices of *The New Republic* to solicit work as a reviewer. He was at that time a rather slender young man, giving no hint of the engaging appearance of a British ship captain closely related to Henry James which he was to have a few years later. It was scarcely a meeting at all, for my admiration, and envy, of Wilson made me shy, and Wilson himself seemed shy: there were just enough years between us to make it possible that he felt the special uneasiness, which I then could not imagine, of the established senior toward the aspiring junior. He politely showed me over the rows and piles of books—those melancholy rows and piles of books in the office of the literary editor, passively waiting to be noticed—and we made no connection whatever. Nor, indeed, did we ever become at all well acquainted after other meetings during the years, but I speak of Wilson in a personal way because he had so personal an effect upon me. He seemed in his own person, and young as he was, to propose and to realize the idea of the literary life.

We are all a little sour on the idea of the literary life these days. The image of the institutionalized intellectual activity of the intellectual capital, of the man of letters in a community of his compeers, no longer pleases and commands us. And very likely there is some good reason for this feeling. But the literary life, apart from the fact that it may have its good pleasures and true rewards, is quite indispensable to civilization, and it isn't a propitious sign that we have become disenchanted with it. In America it has always been very difficult to believe that this life really exists at all or that it is worth living. But for me, and for a good many of my friends, Wilson made it a reality and a very attractive one. He was, of course, not the only good writer of the time, but he seemed to represent the life of letters in an especially cogent way, by reason of the orderliness of his mind and the bold lucidity and simplicity of his prose—lucidity and simplicity of style seemed bold to me even then—and because of the catholicity of his interests and the naturalness with which he dealt with the past as well as with the present. One got from him a whiff of Lessing at Hamburg, of Sainte-Beuve in Paris.

I remember with great distinctness and particular gratitude a specific incident of the personal effect of Wilson's intellectual quality and position. It took place at what I think was our second meeting, which occurred in a men's-room of the New School for Social Research during an intermission at some political affair of the Thirties. At that time "everybody" was involved in radical politics in one degree or another, and Wilson himself was a controversial figure because of his famous statement, made in his essay of 1932, "A Plea to Progressives," that we—that is, the progressives or liberals—should take Communism away from the Communists. I was trying to write a book about Matthew Arnold and having a bitter time of it because it seemed to me that I was working in a lost world, that nobody wanted, or could possibly want, a book about Matthew Arnold. Nor was I being what in those days would have been called "subjective"—no one did want the book. They wanted it even the less because it was to be a doctoral dissertation: there was at that time a great deal of surveillance of the dwelling places of the mind, and ivory towers were very easily imputed; the university, it is true, was just then beginning to figure in people's minds more than ever before in America, but it did not enjoy the prestige, though ambiguous, which it now has, and I was much ashamed of what I had undertaken. But Wilson asked me how my book was getting on, and not merely out of politeness but, as was clear, because he actually thought that a book on Matthew Arnold might be interesting and useful. He wanted to read it. It is impossible to overestimate the liberating effect which this had upon me, the sudden sense that I no longer had to suppose that I was doing a shameful academic drudgery, that I was not required to work with the crippling belief that I was "turning away" from the actual and miserable present to the unreal and comfortable past. The kindest and most intelligent of professors could not possibly have done this for me—it needed Wilson with his involvement in the life of the present which was so clearly not at odds with his natural and highly developed feeling for scholarship.

My first sense of Wilson has remained with me over the intervening years, in which, as is natural, I have found myself sometimes at odds with him. Any reader's relation to a critic is, and ought to be, an uneasy one, and if the reader is himself given to the practice of criticism, he is especially likely to turn a questioning mind on other critics, for he defines himself by the questions he asks and the disagreements he institutes. But in the back-and-forth of critical dialectic it has never occurred to me to alter my first estimate of Wilson's special intellectual quality or my judgment of the peculiar importance of his early work. And the rightness of that judgment is confirmed by *The Shores of Light,* the volume in which Wilson collects his essays and reviews of the Twenties and Thirties. There are things in it which seem to me quite mistaken, as when, to exemplify what he calls the "stuffed-shirt side of Wordsworth," Wilson cites "The Leech-Gatherer," which is surely one of the finest of Wordsworth's poems; or when he speaks of Samuel Butler's "queer intellectual position in attacking Darwin"—there is nothing at all queer about it. But the mistakes do not matter very much—they really never do matter much in a good critic; they may even be an element of his virtue. And Wilson's critical virtue of the Twenties and Thirties is really as large as we remember it to be. The essays and reviews, read thirty or twenty years later, are as serious, as workmanlike, as interested, as interesting, as they ever seemed. This is indeed a considerable achievement, for it is the unhappy characteristic of much work of the same period that it now seems faint and dim, unformed and tiresome.

The Shores of Light bears the subtitle "A Literary Chronicle of the Twenties and Thirties" and in the historiography of the period in which it was written and to which it refers it is a document of first importance. The period is now far enough in the past to justify its being made an object of academic study, and the notions which are held of it by students and by young teachers are often enough of a kind to make one despair of the whole possibility of literary history. Possibly Wilson's collection will do something to correct the gross misapprehensions that prevail. It constitutes the best account of the culture of the period that I know, and what it lacks in system and completeness, it more than compensates for by its intimate and accurate understanding of literary events. No academic history is likely to improve on the simplicity and directness of the understanding which Wilson gives us of such matters as the Humanist controversy, the attitude to the popular arts, the early doctrinaire nationalism of Van Wyck Brooks, the ideas about the relation of literature and politics which flourished after 1929.

Of the ninety pieces which comprise *The Shores of Light,* seventy-three first appeared in *The New Republic,* of which Wilson was for some years the literary editor. We have nothing in our intellectual life today like *The New Republic* of that time, no periodical, generally accepted by the intellectual class, serving both politics and literature on the assumption that politics and literature naturally live in a lively interconnection. After Wilson left the magazine, that assumption began to lose its vitality. It was an idea entirely beyond the comprehension of Bruce Bliven, under whose editorship it quite died. But it was taken for granted in Wilson's day, and the social, political concern of the magazine, however we want to estimate its value in itself, made the perfect context for his literary criticism. The belief in a national moral destiny, which marked liberal social and political opinion after the first war, complemented and gave weight to the sense of a developing American culture.

This social and political context for his criticism was not the only advantage that Wilson derived from his editorial post on *The New Republic.* The authority with which he could speak by right of function as well as by right of talent; the frequency with which, as a matter of duty, his work appeared; the continuity of his writing over a considerable time—these circumstances were of great benefit to him. He was not in the situation of the merely occasional reviewer or essayist, who, if he has anything to say, is likely to say too much and to say it too hard in order to establish his identity and his authority, and this editorial situation of Wilson's had, I think, a decisive effect on his style. In the preface to *The Shores of Light* Wilson apologizes for his frequent use of the first person singular, which, he says, was a prevailing habit of the time even among young and unknown men; but the apology is needless, and the case and number of the pronoun are exactly appropriate to his situation. "I" has its own modesty, and a more impersonal form would not have been suitable to a writer addressing himself regularly to the relatively small and essentially homogeneous group of people who read *The New Republic.* The tone of the pieces of *Classics and Commercials,* most of which appeared in *The New Yorker,* is not so felicitous, chiefly because of Wilson's natural response to the size of the audience and its heterogeneity.

One of the things that must strike the reader of *The Shores of Light* is Wilson's love of books in and for themselves. This has not changed with the years, and it is what made so many of the younger critics, when *Classics and Commercials* appeared two years ago, pass over the critical judgments they disagreed with to speak of their pleasure and relief at Wilson's passion for literature. Of this Wilson himself is aware, and about it he is militant. In 1938 he wrote one of his most amusing parodies, "The Pleasures of Literature," in which he assumed the character of Christopher Morley, a browser among dusty shelves, a devourer of delicious half-forgotten tomes, a reader under hedgerows of delightful, ever-to-be-cherished volumes; in which guise and by which device he made a plea for books in themselves, for *belles lettres* (the very name has become a sneer). In 1938 it was political seriousness and orthodoxy which stood in the way of a love of books, but since that time other seriousnesses and orthodoxies have come to intervene, most especially our seriousness and orthodoxy about literature itself—in the degree that we have come to take literature with an unprecedented, a religious, seriousness, we seem to have lost our pleasure in reading. More and more young people undertake the professional study of literature; fewer and fewer like to read. It is my impression that the act of reading, which used to be an appetite and a passion, is now thought to be rather *infra dig* in people of intelligence; students make it a habit to settle on a very few authors, or, if possible, on one author, whom they undertake to comprehend entirely and to make their own; or to wait until they can conceive a "problem" suitable to their talents before they read at all.

There is indeed something very appealing in Wilson's old-fashioned, undoctrinaire voracity for print. For him a book is a book, the life blood of a spirit which may not be particularly precious but which is likely to be interesting if only for its badness. If one imputes a fault, it is that, while so many spirits are interesting to Wilson, there seem to be not quite enough that are precious. He is certainly far from being without enthusiasm or respect. He has a peculiar gentleness toward writers who are modest or minor. Where his personal feeling toward a writer is involved by reason of friendship, he has a very generous loyalty, as in the memoirs of Christian Gauss and Edna St. Vincent Millay, the two recent essays which form respectively the prologue and epilogue of *The Shores of Light*. But the fullness of his literary feeling is directed toward, as it were, the general enterprise of literature. Toward the individual writer he maintains the attitude of *nil admirare*—by which we are not to understand that he does not admire individual writers, but that he is never astonished by them, or led to surrender himself to them. I speak of this as a fault, yet it is a virtue too, of an astringent kind, at a time when all too often we are inclined to deal with literature as a spiritual revelation, less as writing than as Scripture.

It is Wilson's love of literature in general and his enormous appetite for it in all its forms that must account for his warm sympathy with Saintsbury, a critic in whom I find it hard to discover merit. The two men are of course in many respects at opposite poles from each other. For example, Wilson truly says of Saintsbury that "he had no interest in ideas," and certainly an interest in ideas, although with the years it has become rather less explicit in his work, is of the very essence of Wilson's criticism. Yet we can say of Saintsbury's response to literature that, almost by its very lack of ideas and of interest in ideas, by the very indiscriminateness of its voracity, it expresses an emotion that might seem to pass for an idea—for it affirms the swarming, multitudinous democracy of letters, and testifies to the rightness of loving civilization and culture in and for themselves and of taking pleasure in human communication almost for its own sake and of the order and peace in which men may listen to each other and have time and generosity enough to listen even to those who do not succeed in saying the absolutely best things.

And this idea, if we may call it that, is what chiefly animates the work of Edmund Wilson. It is given explicit expression in an essay which was written as long ago as 1927, "A Preface to Persius." But so early as in that quite moving essay Wilson adds to this "conservative" and "aristocratic" conception of literature an element which was beyond Saintsbury's grasp, the awareness that what constitutes the matter of literature is the discordant and destructive reality that threatens the peace which makes literature possible.

1952

Freud's Last Book

IN JULY of 1938, during his London exile and in the painful last year of his long life, Sigmund Freud set down, in what we now know to be his ultimate formulation, the principles of the science he had created. He did not bring the brief work to an actual conclusion, but its translator is surely right in saying that it cannot be far from its planned end. As we have it, *An Outline of Psychoanalysis* consists of a remarkably clear statement of the psychoanalytical conception of the mind, a succinct explanation of neurosis, and a modest account of the analytical therapy. It breaks off at a point where Freud seems about to engage in moral consideration and cultural generalization.

The little book must be read in the light of its declared intention. It does not undertake to make a contribution of new ideas to psychoanalysis. Nor do its title and its lucid brevity constitute it a primer of the subject. It is not a difficult book, but neither is it elementary; and, as Freud says, it does not intend "to compel belief or to establish conviction." Its aim is simply "to bring together the doctrines of psychoanalysis and to state them, as it were, dogmatically—and in the most concise form and in the most positive terms."

An Outline of Psychoanalysis is to be read, then, as a sort of intellectual last testament of its author. Read so, it can serve as the occasion of a great intellectual, moral, and even aesthetic experience.

What strikes us first in the *Outline* is the style of Freud. Not the literary style merely, though that of course is remarkable, but the whole personal style—the "life-style" of which the literary manner is but one expression.

Our culture inclines to prefer the bland and apologetic intellectual personality and we are set at ease by the self-depreciatory gesture. A kind of corrupt version of the scientific attitude serves to rationalize our wish to believe that one idea is as good as the next, and we like to suppose that a man is wrong in the degree that he is positive. And Freud is always positive—he startles us by seeming to speak as if he had put himself to school to Nature herself and had actually learned something in her fierce seminar.

This is the sign of his intellectual tradition. He liked to insist on his connection with the great pioneering natural scientists of the centuries before our own. Goethe was his acknowledged master and Diderot a kindred spirit, and he shared with these men not only their complex, organic view of the mind but also their vital confidence that mind and Nature could come to some large mutual understanding.

But Freud's positiveness, his belief that truth could actually be found, is also the sign of something particular in his temperament, particular in his vision of the world. It is an aspect of the passion of his response to the pain of life, the mark of his moral urgency, of his deep therapeutic commitment to the human cause.

And this, among other things, makes Freud pre-eminent among the modern theorists of the mind. The antagonists and modifiers of Freud's ideas may be compared among themselves as more or less cogent, but none of them can represent as adequately as Freud the stress and pain of the soul. It is charged against Freud by his opponents that he devaluates human life, that he does not sufficiently respect culture, or art, or love, or women, or the hope of human progress. Yet of those who make the accusation none has yet equaled Freud in actual respect for mankind by equaling him in the full estimation of human suffering or of the forces that cause it.

If we look for an analogue to Freud's vision of life, we find it, I think, in certain great literary minds. Say what we will about Freud's dealings with Shakespeare, his is the Shakespearean vision. And it is not mere accident that he levied upon Sophocles for the name of one of his central concepts.

No doubt the thing we respond to in great tragedy is the implication of some meaningful relation between free will and necessity, and it is what we respond to in Freud. One of the common objections to Freud is that he grants too much to necessity, and that, in doing so, he limits the scope of man's possible development. There is irony in the accusation, in view of the whole intention of psychoanalysis, which is to free the soul from bondage to the necessities that do not actually exist so that it may effectually confront those that do exist. Like any tragic poet, like any true moralist, Freud took it as one of his tasks to define the borders of necessity in order to establish the realm of freedom.

An Outline of Psychoanalysis make abundantly clear how much account of necessity—of what the poet calls fate—Freud does take. He sees man as conditioned and limited by his own nature—by his biological heritage (in the *id*), by his long cultural history (in the *super-ego*). He believes that man in society will always be subject to more or less painful tensions, that what we call neurosis is only a quantitative variation in these tensions, the result of ascertainable causes. Man as Freud conceives him makes his own limiting necessity by being man.

This stern but never hopeless knowledge is precisely the vision of reality that we respond to in tragic art. Freud, when he spoke of the "reality principle," set it in opposition to the "pleasure principle," but the reality principle has its own charge of pleasure, perhaps even in the life of morality, certainly in the life of intellect and art. That is why I have spoken of *An Outline of Psychoanalysis* as being the occasion of an aesthetic experience.

One can respond to Freud with pleasure even when his drive to reality yields unacceptable results. For example, the *Outline* establishes as part of Freud's system an earlier idea of his that was once no more than speculative—it gives to the "death instinct" a place equal in importance to that of the libidinal or creative instinct. The death instinct is a concept rejected by many of even the most thoroughgoing Freudian analysts (as Freud mildly notes); the late Otto Fenichel in his authoritative work on the neurosis argues cogently against it. Yet even if we should be led to reject the theory, we still cannot miss its grandeur, its ultimate tragic courage in acquiescence to fate.

The tragic vision requires the full awareness of the limits which necessity imposes. But it deteriorates if it does not match this awareness with an idea of freedom. Freud undertook to provide such an idea—it was his life work. And if in *An Outline of Psychoanalysis* he insists on the limiting conditions of man's biological and social heritage, yet one of the last sentences of the book is an instigation to the mastery of the hard inheritance. It is a sentence from Goethe: "What you have inherited from your fathers, truly possess it so as to make it your very own."

1949

The Situation of the American Intellectual at the Present Time

THE editors of *Partisan Review* have long been thought to give a rather special credence and sympathy to the idea of "alienation," particularly to the alienation of the modern artist, most of all to the alienation of the American artist. When, therefore, they instituted a symposium on the attitude of American intellectuals toward America at the present time, it was inevitable that a certain significance should be thought to attach to their having proposed the subject at this point in history. To some it seemed to suggest that the editors perceived—and perhaps condoned and even welcomed—a lessening of the degree of alienation which they had observed, and which they had both deplored and cherished. The symposium was called "Our Country and Our Culture," and one of the twenty-four participants found in the use of the possessive pronoun the clear evidence of the end of the fighting spirit in *Partisan Review* and in the whole of the intellectual class—*our* country? *our* culture?—and this attitude was shared in greater or less degree by two other contributors. But the other twenty-one, among whom were the editors themselves, treated the subject on its merits, and most of them were willing to say or imply that they could indeed discover in themselves a diminution of the sense of alienation which at some earlier time they would have taken for granted. No one expressed himself as being enraptured by the cultural situation, but most of those who wrote did seem to be saying that they were truly involved in it, and with some sufficient hope, with some aggressive joy at engaging in the conflict of interests which every reasonably healthy culture is.

The nature of the questions (as well as the nature of the contributors) perhaps made it inevitable that "culture" should be conceived of in a certain way, what might be called an institutional way. In point of fact, of course, when you speak of your degree of alienation, greater or less, you are not responding merely to the chances of making a living as an artist or an intellectual, or to the quality of the books the publishing houses are bringing out, or to the number of art galleries, symphonic orchestras, and literary reviews, or to the state of the universities. These things are no doubt of prime importance, but, as much as to them, when you speak of your relation with your country and your culture, you are responding to a tone and a style in your compatriots, to their tempo of movement, the inflection of their voices, the look on their faces. You trust or you do not trust. You penetrate beneath the manner and the manners to the intention which the manner and manners stand for, you become aware of your compatriots' estimate of the future, of their relation to life and death. Sometimes, as you meditate upon yourself in your individuality, insisting upon that individuality for the moment or for an extended time, your fellow beings simply do not seem very real to you. They do not seem to exist sufficiently. You have lost the power to understand their intentions. Or, if you understand, you are repelled or frightened. At such moments, the people of a foreign nation may become very attractive. Our literary and cultural history is full of the records of romances with other cultures, or, sometimes, with other classes. Haunted as we all are by unquiet dreams of peace and wholeness, we are eager and quick to find them embodied in another people. Other peoples may have for us the same beautiful integrity that, from childhood on, we are taught to find in some period of our national or ethnic pasts. Truth, we feel, must *somewhere* be embodied in man. Ever since the nineteenth century, we have been fixing on one kind of person or another, on one group of people or another, to satisfy our yearning—the peasant and the child have served our purpose; so has woman; so has the worker; for the English, there has been a special value in Italians and Arabs; most nations of Europe have set high store upon the Chinese; Americans have made use of the English, the French rural classes, and Negroes. And so on, everyone searching for innocence, for simplicity and integrity of life.

But there also comes a moment when the faces, the gait, the tone, the manner and manners of one's own people become just what one needs, and the whole look and style of one's culture seems appropriate, seems perhaps not good but intensely *possible*. What your compatriots are silently saying about the future, about life and death, may seem suddenly very accessible to you, and not wrong. You are at a gathering of people, or you are in a classroom, and, being the kind of unpleasant person you are, you know that you might take one individual after another and make yourself fully aware of his foolishness or awkwardness and that you might say, "And this is my country! And this is my culture!" But instead of doing that, you let yourself become aware of something that is really in the room, some common intention of the spirit, which, although it may be checked and impeded, is not foolish or awkward but rather graceful, and not wrong. This can be a very real experience, and just because it can be so real—because, that is, the category of culture is so deeply implanted in the modern mind—it can be easily falsified and must therefore be subjected to critical analysis of the strictest kind. Every country has its false language of at-homeness. The American false language of at-homeness, of contented national consciousness, can be dreadfully boring. Not vicious, just boring. I am not speaking of political chauvinism, but of a kind of cultural idealism that can be served by so decent a man as Stephen Vincent Benét, or by so good a poet as Hart Crane, or by so gifted a person as Thomas Wolfe, not to mention lesser writers than these, not to mention the writers of advertisements. But beyond that false language there really is the possibility of a real feeling, which is likely to express itself in indirect and ironic ways, and critically, and wryly.

Something of this sort of feeling is, I think, at work among American intellectuals at this time. I take occasion to refer to it because, although it was not mentioned by any of the contributors to the *Partisan* symposium, I venture to think that it was actually one of the conditions of their thought. Needless to say, this more intangible aspect of "culture" is not unrelated to the institutional aspects about which the contributors did write.

What follows is what I wrote for the symposium, somewhat expanded in detail. The questions which were put by the *Partisan Review* editors, intended rather to suggest the direction of what was written than to be replied to directly, are these:

1. To what extent have American intellectuals actually changed their attitude toward America and its institutions?

2. Must the American intellectual and writer adapt himself to mass culture? If he must, what forms can his adaptation take? Or, do you believe that a democratic society necessarily leads to a leveling of culture, to a mass culture which will overrun intellectual and aesthetic values traditional to Western civilization?

3. Where in American life can artists and intellectuals find the basis of strength, renewal, and recognition, now that they can no longer depend fully on Europe as a cultural example and a source of vitality?

4. If a reaffimation and rediscovery of America is under way, can the tradition of critical nonconformism (going back to Thoreau and Melville and embracing some of the major expressions of American intellectual history) be maintained as strongly as ever?

It is certainly true that in recent years—say the last ten—American intellectuals have considerably, even radically, revised their attitude toward America. It is no longer the case, as it once used to be, that an avowed aloofness from national feeling is the young intellectual's first ceremonial step into the life of thought.

The ritual of seeming to repudiate one's nation, of denying, in one degree or another, the intellectual and emotional and moral value of the national idea, was not, of course, peculiar to the initiation of the American intellectual. It is part of a tendency of Western culture which developed along with the belief that the national state was in the control and at the service of the *bourgeoisie*. Certainly it was no less common in England than in America, as we know if only through the writings of that remarkable man, George Orwell. Himself an intellectual, and an intellectual of the left, and a man who had little use for conventional notions as such, Orwell nevertheless had a reasoned but strong attachment to the idea of England, and he characterized in a very stringent way those intellectuals who treated this idea with habitual contempt. (As much as anything else, I am sure, it was the mere habituality of the attitude that aroused Orwell's anger.) The gist of his criticism was that the English intellectuals of the left threw out the actuality of social life with the idea of the nation; that they expressed by their anti-nationalism their ignorance of the conditioned nature of all social and political life and their indifference to responsibility; and that, in preferring ideology to nationality, they blinded themselves to the truth that the nation, in the present historical crisis, might represent a principle of freedom as against the tyrannical actuality of any existing ideology.

A prime reason for the change in the American intellectual's attitude toward his nation is of course America's new relation with the other nations of the world. Even the most disaffected American intellectual must nowadays respond, if only in the way of personal interestedness, to the growing isolation of his country amid the hostility which is directed against it. He has become aware of the virtual uniqueness of American security and well-being, and, at the same time, of the danger in which they stand. Perhaps for the first time in his life, he has associated his native land with the not inconsiderable advantages of a whole skin, a full stomach, and the right to wag his tongue as he pleases. (And despite both American and

European belief to the contrary, it is true, and true in a very simple way, that he does have the right to wag his tongue as he pleases.)

He also responds to the fact that there is now no longer any foreign cultural ideal to which he can possibly fly from that American stupidity and vulgarity, the institutionalized awareness of which was once likely to have been the mainspring of his mental life. The ideal of the Workers' Fatherland systematically destroyed itself some time back—even the dullest intellectual now knows better than to choose Kronos for a foster father. Nor can he any longer entertain the ideal of the bright cosmopolis of artists and thinkers, usually localized in Paris.

But the change in the American intellectual's attitude toward his country is not merely the result of his having been driven back to within its borders. The American situation has changed in a way that it not merely relative. There is an unmistakable improvement in the American cultural situation of today over that of, say, thirty years ago. This statement is, of course, much too simple and I make it with the awareness that no cultural situation is ever really good, culture being not a free creation but a continuous bargaining with life, an exchange in which one may yield less or more, but never nothing. Yet as against the state of affairs of three decades ago, we are notably better off.

The improvement is manifold. I shall choose only one aspect of it and remark the change in the relation of wealth to intellect. In many civilizations there comes a point at which wealth shows a tendency to submit itself, in some degree, to the rule of mind and imagination, to apologize for its existence by a show of taste and sensitivity. In America the signs of this submission have for some time been visible. For assignable reasons which cannot be here enumerated, wealth inclines to be uneasy about itself. I do not think that in a commercial civilization the acquisition of money can be anything but a prime goal, but I do think that acquisition as a way of life has become conscious of the effective competition of other ways of life.

And one of the chief competitors is intellect. We cannot, to be sure, put money and mind in entire opposition to each other. At a certain risk—for I know how intellectuals value their perfect purity—I shall advance the idea that the intellect of a society may be thought of as a function of the money of a society, not merely of the wealth in general, but specifically of the money. Like money, intellect is conceptual, critical, and fluent. Where money concentrates, intellect concentrates; and money finds that it needs intellect, just as intellect finds that it needs money. But this symbiosis may at times be attenuated or suspended, or the two parties may not be aware of it, and the appearance, or even the reality, of opposition may develop between them. In such an opposition as formerly obtained in this country, money was the stronger of the parties, and this superiority and the moral anomaly it represents are recorded in every developed literature of the nineteenth and twentieth centuries.

But at the present time the needs of our society have brought close to the top of the social hierarchy a large class of people of considerable force and complexity of mind. This is to be observed in most of the agencies of our society, in, for example, government, finance, industry, journalism. The Luce periodicals have for many years been an established butt of the progressive intellectuals, who hate them for their politics and their pretentiousness. The progressive intellectuals are not entirely wrong in their judgment, yet the fact is that the Luce organizations have always been explicit in their desire for the best possible intellectual talent and have been able, by and large, to satisfy their wish. The use to which this talent is put is not frequently defensible, but I am not arguing the point of intellectual virtue—I am making a neutral sociological observation of the place of intellect in our society. Intellect has associated itself with power, perhaps as never before in history, and is now conceded to be in itself a kind of power. The American populist feeling against mind, against the expert, the theorist, and the brain truster, is no doubt still strong. But it has not prevented the entry into our political and social life of an ever-growing class which we must call intellectual, although it is not necessarily a class of "intellectuals."

The strength of this class, its pervasion through our national life, is indicated by the phenomenon of Governor Stevenson. His defeat in the national election is not to the point, and in any case, it is to be accounted for by very complex causes. What is to the point is that, having avowed himself to be an intellectual (in an almost unduly ostentatious way, with a touch of the intellectual's masochism we know all too well), he yet won the Democratic nomination, aroused enormous enthusiasm, and received a strikingly large popular vote despite the obvious apathy and inefficiency of the Democratic machine. To be sure, Governor Stevenson's tone led his successful opponent to express himself in a manner calculated to appeal to the relatively ignorant and anti-intellectual (a manner, it is to be noted, very different from the admirable one in which he could address an academic audience), and this undoubtedly played its part in General Eisenhower's victory. But I do not for a moment undertake to say that there is not a very large element of our population which responds hostilely to intelligence. Any national population, as Walter Bagehot remarked, is a kind of geological formation of culture in which the most primitive coexists with the most highly developed.

The new intellectual class to which I refer is to be accounted for not only by the growing complexity of the administration of our society but also by the necessity of providing a new means of social mobility. Our many bureaus and authorities, our new employments for people of some trained intellectual capacity, were created not only as a response to the social needs which they serve, but also as a response to the social desires of their personnel. They have the function of making jobs and careers for a large class of people whose minds are their only capital. The social principle here at work may or may not be conscious, but it is omnipresent and very strong; and it would seem to be of the very essence of a modern democracy. It may be observed not only in government but in the policy of the powerful labor unions, which are drawing to themselves and carefully training young college graduates to carry out their increasingly complex undertakings. It is to be observed in the increased prestige of the universities. The university teacher now occupies a place in our social hierarchy which is considerably higher than he could have claimed three decades ago. The academic career is now far more attractive to members of all classes than it used to be. One cannot but be struck by the number of well-to-do students who, presumably with their parents' consent, now elect the academic life, just as one cannot but be struck by the even more significant number of students making the same election who, even ten years ago, would have thought themselves debarred from the academic life by class or ethnic considerations, or who would not have consented to think that the rewards of the academic life, now available to them by reason of the increased social mobility, would have been sufficient compensation for their own efforts or their parents' sacrifices.

My own observation of the new tendency does not give me unalloyed delight. As I look, for example, at the present academic situation, I become aware that the movement toward the university is charged with the special impurity that is to be discovered in the professions which are not in their nature gainful. The motives for the study of the humanities often seem to me to be those of laziness, or indecisiveness, or fear, the fear of the contamination of the brisk world, or the simple desire for the degree of prestige that has newly been attached to the profession. And in general I do not believe that a high incidence of conscious professional intellect in a society necessarily makes for a good culture. It is even possible to imagine that a personnel of considerable intellectual power would have little interest in what is called the intellectual life, and even less interest in art. But this is at present not quite the case. The members of the newly expanded intellectual class that I have been describing, partly by reason of the old cultural sanctions, which may operate only as a kind of snobbery but which still do operate, and partly because they know that the mental life of practical reality does have a relation to the mental life of theory and free imagination, are at least potentially supporters and consumers of high culture. They do not necessarily demand the best, but they demand what is called the best;

they demand something. The dreadful haste and overcrowding of their lives prevents them from getting as much as they might want and need. So does the stupidity of the entrepreneurs of culture, such as publishers, who, in this country, have not had a new idea since they invented the cocktail party.* So does the nature of the commitment of most of the people who produce the cultural commodity, that is, the actual "intellectuals." Yet it seems to me that art and thought are more generally and happily received and recognized—if still not wholly loved—than they have ever been in America.

A country like ours, as big as ours, compounded of so many elements of a heterogeneous sort, makes it difficult for us to think that ideas such as might be entertained by anything resembling an elite can have any direct influence in the country at large. And it is undoubtedly true that there is a considerable inertia that must be taken into account as we calculate the place of mind in our national life. But we should be wrong to conclude that the inertia is wholly definitive of our cultural situation. This is a characteristic mistake of the American intellectual, particularly the literary intellectual, with whom I am naturally most concerned. His sense of an inert American mass resistant to ideas, entirely unenlightened, and hating enlightenment, is part of the pathos of liberalism in the Twenties and Thirties, which is sedulously maintained despite the fact that the liberal ideas of the Twenties and Thirties are, I will not say dominant—this might, at the present juncture of affairs, be misleading—but strong and established, truly powerful. That the resistance to these ideas often takes an ugly, mindless form I should not think of denying, but this must not blind us to the power of ideas among us, to the existence of a very considerable class which is moved by ideas.

The literary intellectual is likely to be unaware of this, because he is ignorant of the channels through which opinion flows. He does not, for example, know anything about the existence and the training and the influence of, say, high-school teachers, or ministers, or

* In 1956 I must modify this harsh statement about publishers by taking note of the remarkable new phenomenon of the paper-bound book.

lawyers, or social workers, the people of the professions whose stock in trade is ideas of some kind. Nor does he have any real awareness of the ideas which pass current among these people, or the form in which they are found acceptable. He is likely to think of ideas, of "real" ideas as being limited to the most highly developed, the most "advanced," the most esoteric ideas that he himself is capable of absorbing and of finding aesthetic pleasure in. And when he tests society for the presence of the ideas to which he gives his attention, he finds what he expects to find—no, they are not present, or they are not present in the form in which he knows them. But ideas of some kind, and by no means of a bad or retrograde kind, are indeed present.

I was able to make my own test of this when I recently had occasion to meet with two groups, one of high-school teachers, the other of men concerned in a professional way with the revision of our penal code. In both cases, I ought to say, the participants were the best of their professions—the teachers having been selected for fellowships in leading universities, the penal group consisting of professors of law, judges, psychiatrists, and penologists—yet they did not, I ought also to say, by any means comport themselves as isolated and desperate minorities but rather as people who, by their choice among ideas and their avowed intention of making them prevail, could effect change and make improvements in the conduct of their professions. And my sense of the seriousness of these people, of their commitment to ideas, of their willingness to examine ideas, my sense of their appropriate intellectual humility, by which I mean their willingness to test ideas by experience and by the criterion of human welfare, was to me what it should not have been, a revelation. Should not have been: for to the literary intellectual any profession other than that of literature condemns itself by the mere fact of its being a profession.

From what I have said about the increased power of mind in the nation, something of my answer to the question about mass culture may be inferred. Although mass culture is no doubt a very considerable threat to high culture, there is a countervailing condition in the class I have been describing. As for mass culture itself, one never knows, of course, what may happen in any kind of cultural situation. It is possible that mass culture, if it is not fixed and made static, might become a better thing than it now is, that it might attract genius and discover that it has an inherent law of development. But at the moment I am chiefly interested in the continuation of the traditional culture in the traditional forms. I am therefore concerned with the existence and effect of the large intellectual elite I have described. This group will not be—is not—content with mass culture as we now have it, because for its very existence it requires new ideas, or at the least the simulacra of new ideas.

The social complexion of the new large intellectual class which I have been hypostasizing must be taken fully into account as we estimate the cultural situation it makes. The intellectual and quasi-intellectual classes of contemporary America characteristically push up from the bottom. They are always new. Very little is taken for granted by them. Very little can be taken for granted in instructing them or in trying to influence them. They have, as it were, only a very small cultural reserve. In some ways this is deplorable, making it difficult to think of the refinement of ideas, making it almost impossible to hope for grace and vivacity in the intellectual life. But in some ways it is an advantage, for it assures for the intellectual life a certain simplicity and actuality, an ever-renewed energy of discovery.

From my sense of this there follows my answer to the question: where in American life can the artists and intellectuals find the basis of strength, renewal, and recognition, now that they can't depend on Europe as a cultural example?

In attempting an answer, I shall not speak of the artist, only of the intellectual. For purposes of the artist's salvation, it is best not to speak of the artist at all. It is best to think of him as crazy, foolish, inspired—as an unconditionable kind of man—and to make no provision for him until he appears in person and demands it. Our attitude to the artist is deteriorating as our sense of his need increases.

It seems to me that the more we think about doing something for the artist, the less we think of him as Master, and the more we think of him as Postulant or Apprentice. Indeed, it may be coming to be true that for us the Master is not the artist himself, but the great philanthropic Foundation, which brings artists into being, whose creative act the artist is. All the signs point toward our desire to institutionalize the artist, to integrate him into the community. By means of university courses which teach the "technique" of writing, or which arrange for the communication of the spirit from a fully initiated artist to the neophyte, by means of doctoral degrees in creativity, by means of summer schools and conferences, our democratic impulses fulfill themselves and we undertake to prove that art is a profession like another, in which a young man of reasonably good intelligence has a right to succeed. And this undertaking, which is carried out by administrators and by teachers of relatively simple mind, is in reality the response to the theory of more elaborate and refined minds—of intellectuals—who conceive of the artist as the Commissioner of Moral Sanitation, and who demand that he be given his proper statutory salary without delay. I do not hold with the theory that art grows best in hardship. But I become uneasy—especially if I consider the nature of the best of modern art, its demand that it be wrestled with before it consents to bless us—whenever I hear of plans for its early domestication. These plans seem to me an aspect of the modern fear of being cut off from the social group even for a moment, of the modern indignation at the idea of entering the life of the spirit without proper provision having been made for full security.

But intellectuals are in a different case. It is possible that plans can be made for their welfare without diminishing their function. They can be trained. They can, I believe, be taught to think, or at least to think better. It is not improper to discuss what kind of work they should be doing, and their manner of doing it, and the conditions of their doing it, and the influences to which they might submit.

In a way it is wrong, or merely academic, to talk of the *influence* of European thought on American thought, since the latter is continuous with the former. But in so far as the American intellectual conceived of the continuity as being an influence, it no doubt was exactly that, and, in being that, it was, in its time, useful. If that influence has now come to an end, we must truly regret the reasons for its termination, we must be sad over what it may suggest of a diminution of free intercourse, of which we can never have enough. And yet it seems to me that if the European influence, as a large, definitive, conscious experience of the American intellectual, has indeed come to an end, this is, at the moment, all to the good.

For the fact is that the American intellectual never so fully expressed his provincialism as in the way he submitted to the influence of Europe. He was provincial in that he thought of culture as an abstraction and as an absolute. So long as Marxism exercised its direct influence on him, he thought of politics as an absolute. So long as French literature exercised its direct influence upon him, he thought of art as an absolute. To put it another way, he understood himself to be involved primarily with the discipline he had elected. To be sure, the times being what they were, he did not make the mistake of supposing that the elected discipline was not connected with reality. But the reality that he conceived was abstractly conceived, or it was conditioned by circumstances which were more specifically local than the American intellectual could quite perceive.

The "society" which the American intellectual learned about from Europe was in large part a construct of Marxism, or a construct of the long war of the French intellectuals with the French *bourgeoisie*. Ideas, of course, are transferrable: there was no reason why the American intellectual might not have transferred to America what he had learned from Europe, why he should not have directed the impatience, the contempt, the demand, the resistance, which are necessary elements of the life of the critical intellect—and, as I think, of a large part of the creative life as well—upon the immediate, the local, the concrete phenomena of American life. I do not say that he did not display impatience, contempt, demand, and resistance, but only that he did not direct them where they should have gone, that he was general and abstract where he should have been specific and concrete. His sense of himself as an intellectual, his conception of the function of criticism, led him always away from the variousness and complexity of phenomena to an abstract totality of perception which issued in despair or disgust, to which he attached a very high degree of spiritual prestige.

The literary mind, more precisely the historical-literary mind, seems to me the best kind of critical mind that we have, better than the theological, better than the philosophical, better than the scientific and the social-scientific. But the literary intellectuals of today, possibly because they are still fascinated by certain foreign traditions, do not look at our culture with anything like the precise critical attention it must have. If we are to maintain the organic pluralism we have come to value more highly than ever before, it is not enough to think of it in its abstract totality—we must be aware of it in its multifarious, tendentious, competitive details.

For example, it is a truism that universal education is one of the essential characteristics of modern democracy and that the quality and content of the education provided is a clear indication of the quality and tendency of the democracy that provides it. What, then, is the condition of American education? The question has been allowed to fall into the hands of reactionaries of the most vicious kind, and of progressives and liberals whose ideas must evoke sympathy and whose goals are probably right in general, but who live in a cave of self-commiseration into which no ray of true criticism ever penetrates. Who among the intellectuals really knows what is being taught in the great teachers' colleges, which have not only great doctrinal influence but also a very considerable practical control of the schools? Those of us who have any awareness of these colleges at all are likely to hold them in contempt because of what we suppose to be their anti-intellectualism, their emphasis on "method" as against "content," or because of their foolish language of "areas" and "frames of reference" and "implementation," or because of their statistical preoccupations, or because of their absurd claims for their profession which lead them to say such things as that education is coextensive with life. Our impression is probably a just one, yet we can by no means be sure. It may be that they are making foolish formulations of something that they perceive with sufficient accuracy. They are in touch with the matrix of our culture; perhaps their theories do not wholly misrepresent what they see there. In one way or another, we who are intellectuals go back in our tradition of schooling to Colet or Dr. Boyer, by which I do not mean to imply that we have been trained in the classical languages, but that at some point or other in our careers, often in the face of our actual schooling, we have submitted ourselves to learning, to what is called a "discipline." But the teachers' colleges may have become aware that the very idea of submission to a discipline is deeply repugnant to the modern American personality, so that any drill or memorizing (which is necessary for certain kinds of learning) is impossible, and all teaching must depend upon "interest" and must have as its goal not knowledge but "attitudes." Or it is possible that the teachers' colleges have discovered that so many agencies in our culture have failed to provide children with the material of an adequate ethos that it really does devolve upon the schools to make the provision.

If my suppositions are true, they involve the idea of a crisis in culture being dealt with by intellectual agencies of considerable magnitude and power—why should not the intellectuals be concerned with it? Yet it scarcely enters our consciousness, except when one of the Luce periodicals makes one of its heedless and malicious attacks on John Dewey, who, in the demonology of the Luce editors, is the particular imp responsible for virtually every fault of American schooling. And yet, although I would not mitigate the characterization of these attacks as heedless and malicious, they do at least suggest a recognition of the importance of ideas in a democracy.

We know nothing of the directives that are issued by the superintendents of the great school systems. Most of us are not aware that these directives are based on the most elaborate theories of society and the individual. Who among us has any adequate idea about the quality of the teaching staffs of the schools? What is the literary curriculum of our high schools? What is taught in "Social Studies"? What actually happens in a "progressive" school—I mean apart from what everybody jokes about? What happens in colleges? These are questions which the intellectuals have been content to leave to the education editor of the *New York Times*. With the result that Dr. Benjamin Fine, a man with, properly enough, his own ax to grind and his own tears to shed, is far more influential in our culture than any intellectual who reads this, or writes it, is ever likely to be.

Psychology is a science to which literary intellectuals feel a natural affinity. But who knows just what is happening in psychology? Dr. Fromm, and the late Dr. Horney, and the late Dr. Sullivan, and their disciples, have great influence upon many members of the elite. What actually do they say? What is the worth of what they say? Their theories, like the theories of the teachers' colleges, are a response, and, I suspect, a subtle response, to the American cultural personality. I suspect that they are responding to the American feeling that things cannot possibly be as bad as that, i.e., as bad as Freud says they are, or as deeply rooted in biology, that if we could only get together and talk over our attitudes and social arrangements, and revise our culture a little, things would be ever so much better and there would be less neurosis and no wars. But what intellectual takes the time to take these theories seriously?* All literary intellectuals know enough about Dr. Wilhelm Reich to gossip about his theories of sexuality. But nowhere have I read a considered critical examination of what he says. Nor are there any signs of late years that the ethics of sexuality is to be considered a serious subject. What is happening to the development of Freud's ideas by those who are called orthodox Freudians? I speak under correction but I suspect that very little

* In 1956, this question can no longer be asked with the expectation of receiving only the implied answer. Several intellectuals have recently written studies of various schools of psychoanalytical thought.

indeed is happening and I regret this very much. One result of what I have come to believe to be the otiosity of the Freudian psychoanalyst is that the intellectual public has withdrawn its sympathy—and its understanding—from the Freudian ideas. For a good many years now I have assigned *Civilization and Its Discontents* to one or another group of students, and I can report how the response to the book has deteriorated from the puzzled respect of some years ago to the present blithe, facetious dismissal. Again and again the public is told, and is very content to hear, that we have got well beyond Freud's possibly useful but certainly primitive and limiting ideas. In point of fact, we have not yet made a beginning in the realization of these ideas—Freud's doctrine has been with us for nearly fifty years and it contains the elements of a most complex moral system, yet I know of no attempt to deal seriously with its implications, or even a true awareness of their existence. Meanwhile the Bollingen Foundation, at considerable expense, is asking us to admire Jung's discovery—made, as it happens, a century ago by a general of the American Army*—that the alchemists were men of the profoundest wisdom, concerned not with the transmutation of metals but of psychic and moral qualities. Jung continues, I believe, to have influence among some sections of the intellectual population; yet, although we do have the admirable, acidulous book of the English Freudian, Dr. Glover, I know of no American who has ventured to deal critically with him except for the tireless Mr. Parelhof, who has made it his life work to demonstrate that Jung's relations with Nazism and his stand on anti-Semitism do him no credit.

Departments of psychology in the universities are detaching themselves from the faculties of philosophy in order to enter the faculties of pure science, on the ground that their science is wholly experimental. What is the value of the very considerable vested interests of this academic psychology? We are as little equipped to give an an-

---

* See *Ethan Allen Hitchcock: Soldier, Humanitarian, Scholar, Discoverer of the "True Subject" of the Hermetic Art*, by I. Bernard Cohen (American Antiquarian Society, Worcester, Massachusetts, 1952).

swer as the laboratory rats themselves. Colleges nowadays give courses in Marriage and Sex, and who knows what is the received doctrine in these courses, let alone in what tone of voice it is delivered?

I could go on with my question at very great length, for I have chosen my two examples pretty much at random from an inexhaustible number. But there is no need for me to go on. My simple point is surely plain. As I make it, I see that it answers the last question which the editors put, about how a reaffirmation and rediscovery of America can go hand in hand with the tradition of critical nonconformism. The editors, to identify the great American tradition of critical nonconformism, speak of it as "going back to Thoreau and Melville." I am glad that they have done so, for it saves me the trouble of defending myself from those to whom it will seem that I recommend an elaborate prostitution of the literary mind to trivialities, to whom it will seem that I have suppressed and betrayed art by my emphasis on the local particularities of culture, and if not art, which I expressly exempted from consideration, then those larger and finer and more transcendent matters to which the most gifted intellectuals are naturally drawn. I think I should be rather more sensitive to the possibility of this rebuke were I aware that in the larger and finer and more transcendent matters the most gifted intellectuals were as knowledgeable and eager as I would wish them to be in grosser and more immediate things. But although everybody knows that there is "a great interest in religion" among American literary intellectuals, I see very little evidence of acquaintance with the documents of religion, except those provided by Graham Greene, and very little confrontation of the actuality of religion; nor do American literary intellectuals give any signs of responsiveness either to music or the plastic arts.

Whatever the particular facts of our cultural situation may turn out to be, the recollection of Thoreau and Melville will sustain me in my certitude that the kind of critical interest I am asking the literary intellectual to take in the life around him is a proper interest of the literary mind, and that it is the right ground on which to approach transcendent things. More: it is the right ground for the literary art to grow in—the right ground for satire, for humor, for irony, for tragedy, for the personal vision affirming itself against the institutional with the peculiar passionateness of art. Art, strange and sad as it may be to have to say it again, really is the criticism of life.

1952/1953

A Novel in Passing

C VIRGIL GHEORGHIU'S novel of wartime and postwar
Europe, *The Twenty-fifth Hour,* is an important book not
because of its intrinsic virtues—it has none—but because of
what it tells us of the political mind of Europe, particularly of
France. In France, the book has had a success that is more remarkable for its kind than for its extent. That *The Twenty-fifth Hour*
should have sold widely is not surprising, for although it is in every
way inferior to Koestler's *Darkness at Noon,* to Camus's *The
Plague,* and to Orwell's *Nineteen Eighty-four,* with all of which it
has been compared, it is, like them, a representation of the modern
apocalypse and therefore recommends itself to the natural apprehension of many readers. But what is indeed surprising is the response it
has won from the French intellectual classes. It has been made the
occasion not only of innumerable articles in the press but also of
great public meetings, elaborate conferences, and episcopal sermons.
It has become, it would seem, something very like a political gospel,
and its author is apparently regarded as a political holy man.

This reception can scarcely be accounted for by the literary power
of *The Twenty-fifth Hour,* or by the quality of its moral feeling, or
by its intellectual cogency. As a novelist Mr. Gheorghiu is never
better than mediocre. His frequent flights of satiric fancy are commonplace. His invective is not passionate, only febrile or petulant.
And even his narrative of man's systematic inhumanity to man, to
which the greater part of the book is devoted, does not succeed in

conveying the actuality of horror. The narrative deals with the fate of two Rumanians, of whom one is a peasant, the other a novelist. The peasant, Johann Moritz, for the personal reasons of the police officer of his village, is classified as a Jew and sent to a Jewish work camp. He escapes to Hungary with a group of his fellow-prisoners who victimize, snub, and desert him, is tortured by the Hungarian police as a Rumanian spy, then sent to Germany with a contingent of slave labor, discovered by a Nazi racial expert to be a member of the purest branch of the Aryan race, and promptly enlisted in the S.S. The climax of his misfortunes comes at the end of the war, when he makes his way to the Americans, who, unaware of his political innocence, put him in a detention camp. Here his fate is presently joined with that of the other Rumanian, the novelist Traian Koruga, whose purity of heart seems to exceed even that of the simple Johann but who is nevertheless being held by the Americans because he had been a member of the Rumanian diplomatic corps. The physical and spiritual brutality of the Americans confirms Koruga in the belief he has propounded in a novel called *The Twenty-fifth Hour*— that the West has reached the hour after the last, "the hour when mankind is beyond salvation." After expressing his rage and despair in a series of satirical protests, he contrives his death by pretending to escape. This is obviously not a narrative that can have anything like the concentrated power of the elaborate and precise fables by which Koestler, Camus, and Orwell have represented the extremity of the modern situation. Indeed, as Mr. Gheorghiu tells it, his story makes only a conventional appeal to the emotions. Far from forcing upon us an appalled realization of the dreadfulness of the recent past, it leads us to ask whether things were not really much worse than Mr. Gheorghiu says they were.

This is in part the result of a literary inadequacy, but it is also the result of an inadequacy of moral sensitivity; one reason Mr. Gheorghiu's picture of the European horror falls short of the truth is that its deals in so minimal and perverse a way with the extreme example of that horror, the fate of the Jews. The American publishers of *The Twenty-fifth Hour* have prepared an account of the author's life in which we are told that when he was once rebuked for not having included in his book any mention of the Jewish extermination camps. Mr. Gheorghiu replied by insisting on the autobiographical nature of his novel—he had not been imprisoned in such a camp and therefore he had not described one. The answer is not acceptable from a man who has taken it upon himself to show, in a work of the imagination, the total depravity of the West, which, he says, has placed it beyond the hope of salvation. Nor, of course, is the reply supported by his book, for if Koruga's adventures are autobiographical, Johann's are not. Furthermore, there are incidents in Johann's adventures that seem calculated to suggest that although the Jews of Europe were certainly involved in the general horror, they managed, when put to it, to rub along pretty well, exploiting the peasants to the last and coming out on the side of the victors.

The American publishers make a great point of telling us that Koruga represents Mr. Gheorghiu in all the circumstances of his life except his martyr's death, and that Koruga's wife is Mr. Gheorghiu's wife. It is really quite hard to guess what is supposed to be gained for the moral authority of the book by this insistence. For Koruga, of whom it is eventually said that he is a saint, had lived very comfortably in the highest official circles of Fascist Rumania and had been able to command for himself a post as cultural attaché at one of its legations. He had responded to the grim events of the time to the extent of writing a novel that explained why salvation was impossible, and he had gone so far in the service of justice and humanity as to try to win Johann's release by proving that Johann was really not a Jew. But he is moved to passion and protest only when he himself suffers imprisonment by the Americans. We certainly cannot condone such behavior as Mr. Gheorghiu attributes to the American military government. But if Koruga is Mr. Gheorghiu, then Mr. Gheorghiu does not quite have the moral authority to deny all hope to the West because the Americans were slow to perceive the true and saintly nature of a man who had lately been a Rumanian diplomat. As for Mrs. Koruga, in order to maintain her position in Rumania, she had been at desperate pains to conceal her Jewish parentage and to destroy the evidence of it. *The Twenty-fifth Hour* does not gain in moral impressiveness because at its end it is she who is made to speak the last high words of European humanism in its stand against the oncoming bleak American future.

And the intellectual quality of *The Twenty-fifth Hour* is of a kind with its literary and moral quality. The sum of Mr. Gheorghiu's political wisdom is a conjunction of two of the stalest clichés of our time—the indiscriminate hatred of technology as the cause of all our ills, and the total rejection of the political life in favor of the individual life of the spirit. Mr. Gheorghiu makes it a strange axiom of history that all masters have had to learn the language of their slaves; modern man, he says, has so thoroughly learned the language of his great multitude of machine slaves that he has forgotten the human tongue, the language of faith and the heart. Hence the modern inability to judge save by quantity; hence, too, the modern cruelty. Mr. Gheorghiu is not checked in his triumphant exposition of this dull and inaccurate idea by any historical recollection, although a native of Rumania, a nation whose history is peculiarly marked by cruelty, should have recalled that, say, Vlad the Impaler reigned in an age of faith and that only a very primitive technology existed at a time when, by the bloodiest means, the masses of Rumanian people were kept in the most extreme subjection. Yet in the face of such obvious considerations, Mr. Gheorghiu goes on to tell us that modern men have sunk to the level of *citizens,* and the citizen, we are told, is "the most dangerous wild beast that has appeared on the face of the earth since the cross between man and the mechanical slave."

Political ideas as feeble as these can scarcely of themselves have taken in a philosopher like Gabriel Marcel, who wrote the introduction for the French version of *The Twenty-fifth Hour,* or a political thinker like Bertrand de Jouvenel, who praises it as a noble book. But it is understandable that Mr. Gheorghiu should have captured these and other good minds by striking below the level of rational criticism to the fear and perplexity of French political life. We in America, bad as we believe things to be with the West, can see that Mr. Ghoerghiu's declaration of the impossibility of hope is factitious, an expression of his own intense self-reference, a way of giving a desperate force to his dull ideas. It comes to us as no surprise to learn that he is relenting and writing a book called *The Second Chance.* But to the French, Mr. Gheorghiu's despair does not seem false and merely literary, for they, alas, are now in the habit of despair. They believe that their political future is no longer perfectly autonomous but is linked either to Russia or to America, and they wish to believe that the choice between the two great powers is no choice at all. A large part of the activity of their intellectual classes consists of demonstrating that the difference between American culture and Russian culture is not to be discerned save as a difference in barbarisms that cannot really command a preference. This is not true, but it is natural that the French should want to think it true. And since they believe they must choose, and since self-esteem works as it does, it is natural that they should insist that the brighter, or at least the more comfortable, of the two alternatives, the American one, is really the more destructive of the qualities they like to think are peculiarly their own. So they respond extravagantly to the intention of Mr. Gheorghiu's book, the real intention, which is not so much to show that the West has been destroyed by the evils of technology and politics as to show that the West is being brought to final ruin by America.

For *The Twenty-fifth Hour* by no means holds the nations of the West equally guilty of the murder of the human spirit—Rumania and Hungary are only somewhat guilty, in a passive way; Germany is of course very guilty, but mad and comical; England is not mentioned; France is left out of the circle of culpability. Russia is denounced for its theory of government and for the barbarousness of its soldiery, but the Russians, bad as they may be, are observed abstractly and from a distance, and it is the Americans who are seen at first hand and in detail as violators of the body and the spirit, torturers of priests, deniers of saints, self-deceiving tempters who seduce mankind with chocolate and warm clothing. What is more, even the best of them, the men of good family and university education, wear no garters, and their socks fall around their ankles and offensively expose bare skin when they cross their legs; they do not remove their cigarettes from their mouths when they shake hands with ladies. This is the unhappy observation of Traian Koruga's widow, who, as the book draws to its end, takes her husband's place as the representative of true humanity, the old European humanity, against depraved technology. And when a poor Lieutenant Lewis ventures to offer marriage to Mrs. Koruga, she promptly confronts him with two great truths. The first is that, for a European lady, marriage to an American is inconceivable, because she is used to the high ideality of European romantic love, which holds that the beloved woman is unique, even absolute, and that her being unattainable is a recognized reason for suicide, while to an American a woman is a woman like another. Upon this follows the presumably corollary truth that the approaching war between America and Russia is merely a conflict between two branches of the same technological culture. It is, says Mrs. Koruga, a truth all Europeans recognize. They may choose American material comfort, but they understand that they are merely preferring one death of the spirit to another.

So there we are. It is to this picture of ourselves as the deadly climax of the modern fate that the French respond when they so extravagantly praise *The Twenty-fifth Hour* and organize political and religious meetings around it. Knowing as we do the distractedness of Europe, this can only make us sad, not indignant. Recognizing our own shortcomings, we can even admit that they might serve as the subject of a noble indictment—what is perhaps the unhappiest aspect of the reception of Mr. Gheorghiu's novel is that the French literary sense should have deteriorated to a point where it can be satisfied with so ignoble a monument to American error.

1950

Two Notes on David Riesman

DAVID RIESMAN'S *The Lonely Crowd* seems to me one of the most important books about America to have been published in recent times. And quite apart from the particularity of its subject, it is one of the most interesting books I have ever read.

This is very large praise, and as I write it I find myself wondering whether I may not be overstating the case for this sociological study in order to counteract the antagonisms to the social sciences which I know to be pretty common among people who like literature very much. But I do not think I am saying more than I mean. My opinion was formed before I ever thought of writing about Mr. Riesman's book and I have tested it by more than one reading.

Yet since I have raised the question of the literary suspiciousness of the social sciences, especially sociology, it might be well to take it specifically into account in connection with *The Lonely Crowd*.

One reason for this suspiciousness is that sociology tends to use a kind of language which must arouse antagonism in people who are at all sensitive to language. This is not because the language of sociology is scientific but because it is often pseudo-scientific and jargonistic and has the effect of giving a false value to ideas that are simple and platitudinous. To any such charge *The Lonely Crowd* is certainly not liable. Mr. Riesman uses two terms that some might boggle at—he speaks of people as being "inner-directed" and "other-directed." But I do not know how else he could denominate the two categories of character that are essential to his thought. In general the book is precisely a work of literature in the old comprehensive sense of the word according to which Hume's essays are literature, or Gibbon's history, or Tocqueville's *Democracy in America*.

Another objection is that sociology is likely to be tendentious without admitting it is, and that it proceeds on unexamined assumptions while insisting that it is wholly objective. But we can count on Mr. Riesman's objectivity because he admits his subjectivity and the hypothetical nature of his enterprise. He is under no illusion of scientific neutrality. He admires certain human qualities and makes no bones about wanting them to be influential in our national life.

Then it is said, and with justice, that sociology often gives the appearance of denying personal autonomy. What is more, much sociological investigation has for its avowed aim the discovery of how to manipulate human behavior in clandestine ways. But Mr. Riesman's book is as far as it can be from denying the possibility of autonomy without denying the inescapable limits of civilized society. Its whole effort, indeed, is directed toward the affirmation of the possibility of autonomy.

People of literary inclinations, I believe, have a natural jealousy of sociology because it seems to be in process of taking over from literature one of literature's most characteristic functions, the investigation and criticism of morals and manners. Yet it is but fair to remark that sociology has pre-empted only what literature has voluntarily surrendered. Twenty years ago, when the Lynds produced their famous study, *Middletown,* it was possible to say that with all their staff and paraphernalia they had not really told us more about American life than we had learned from a solitary insightful observer, which is what some sociologists call a novelist—they had done no more than confirm *Babbitt* by statistics. Since that time, however, few novelists have added anything genuinely new to our knowledge of American life. But the sociologists have, and Mr. Riesman, writing with a sense of social actuality which Scott Fitzgerald might have envied, does literature a service by suggesting to the novelists that there are new and wonderfully arable social fields for them to till.

The research from which *The Lonely Crowd* developed began as an investigation of the social causes of political attitudes, specifically that of apathy to politics. The book does not consist of conclusions drawn from this research but was written in the course of the still continuing enterprise as the hypothesis on which the research might proceed. In its simplest form this hypothesis consists of the statement that there has been a change in the character of the American people, that where once men whose character was "inner-directed" were dominant in our culture, the tendency is now toward the dominance of men of "other-directed" character. Inner-directed persons are those who internalize adult authority, most notably the ideals and demands of their parents. Other-directed persons are those whose character is formed chiefly by their contemporaries and peers, the formation beginning as soon as they enter social life in play or at school.

Something of the nature of the inner-directed man may be understood from the phrase which, in the nineteenth century, he so often made his motto—"*Ad astra per aspera,*" through difficulties to the seemingly unattainable heights. The old tag might also be translated, "To the heights by means of asperity," for a kind of asperity marks the dealings of the inner-directed man with the world, his fellow-men, and himself. The man of business as well as the scientific or artistic genius, or the religious leader, or the philosopher, were all at one in their submission to inner-direction. The belief that energy, self-control, and self-reverence would achieve miracles was held not only by the dullest spirits of the age but also by the noblest. We must think of the Alger books as being the expression not merely of a strenuous philistinism but of a general culture in which strenuousness was valued in all walks of life. There was a connection between the passions of a Bounderby and a Beethoven.

In America, even as far back as Tocqueville's visit, there was always a tendency for inner-direction to be modified by what Tocqueville regarded as an extravagant awareness of the opinion of others.

Emerson believed that this tendency constituted a prime threat to the American spirit and he never wearied of warning his countrymen that Self Reliance—his name for inner-direction—was sadly on the wane. Yet in nineteenth-century America the "hardness of the material" still called for a large measure of inner-direction— there were still frontiers to be conquered, social forms to be imposed or broken, technology to be established. It was still useful to idealize "faith," the belief that one's personal vision was right no matter how the world mocked it. School children were assiduously taught in their readers that the heroic man was one who followed his gleam, and that society as a whole was likely to be stupid, retrograde, and cowardly, as witness its treatment of Columbus. And in the poem that every child learned, it was right of Columbus, and not arrogant or undemocratic of him, to say, "Sail on! Still on!" when his men begged him to turn back. To be "misunderstood," to be alone with one's rightness and virtue, was the stuff of the dreams of youth.

But in the early years of the twentieth century—around 1920, Mr. Riesman believes—the inner-directed character began to lose its ascendancy. The hard, resistant materiality of the world no longer supplied the goal and validated the hard, strenuous will of inner-directed people. Children were less impelled to establish the old parental authority within themselves—parents were less certain of how to establish it in their children and of whether it ought to be established at all. It was by no means clear that the old standards applied to the new kind of work. For in the degree that work had less to do with *things,* it had more to do with *people.* In Mr. Riesman's phrase, the interest shifted from the hardness of the material to the softness of the personnel, and the arts of personality, by which one could manipulate one's fellows or win valuable approval from them, became more important to more people than the direct force of the will exerted upon material difficulties. And children increasingly formed their characters according to the demands of their playmates and schoolmates, equipping themselves with a quick, unconscious sensitivity to the judgment of others—they became increasingly other-directed.

The evidence of this new means of character-formation is manifest in every discussion of juvenile or adolescent social behavior, in which it is always taken for granted that parents are virtually helpless before the power of the child-society. And indeed this power is supported and rationalized by the family and the school, which, on theories of normality and adjustment, second the anxious antagonism which the child-society directs upon any show of difference. For the group life of contemporary children achieves its particular kind of democracy by suppressing special interests and abilities (except in athletics) and by prohibiting the display of vanity or ambition. Even before the child is ready for sociability, his life in literature has prepared him for social adjustment and conformity. *Scuffy the Tugboat* instructs him in the dangers of the Columbus principle, while *Tootle the Engine* leads him to believe that he must not fail to be like all the other little engines and never leave the track to stray into green fields, like a horse.

The ideal of behavior which is indigenous to the social life of the modern child is the model and perhaps the mold of the ideal of adults, at least of the middle class. We are coming to be a civilization in which overt ambition, aggression, and competition are at a discount. Not, of course, that the sources of natural aggression are drying up or that people no longer seek prestige. But self-aggrandizement takes new forms as the ideals of other-direction become increasingly compelling. Overt ambition gives way to what Mr. Riesman calls antagonistic co-operation, which implies affability, blandness, a lively sensitivity to the opinion of the group, the suppression of asperity. Social differences must be minimized as far as possible. Wealth must depreciate itself, and must seek to express itself not in symbols of power but in fineness of taste. Food is ordered less for the old-fashioned virtues of substantiality and abundance, than for the new charms of elegance and artistry—but in this limited space it is impossible to follow Mr. Riesman in the fascinating detail of his description of the cultural changes which other-direction is instituting.

The general opinion is not likely to be in accord with Mr. Riesman—the general opinion is that our culture is marked by an especially fierce and open competitiveness, an unmasked aggressiveness, a crude assertiveness. This is the received idea of a great deal of our literature and of our progressive social thought. It is the pious certainty of Europe, constituting, one sometimes feels, the larger part of the European social and political thought of the moment. And Mr. Riesman's students at the University of Chicago tell him that American life resembles the grim, paranoid Dobu culture or the competitive conspicuously-consuming Kwakiutl culture—none ever finds any resemblance to the peaceable, co-operative Pueblo Indians, although *all* of them wish they could.

I am sure that it is Mr. Riesman who is in the right of the matter. My own experience in teaching confirms his, one incident in particular. For some time I had been increasingly aware that my students had no very great admiration for Stendhal's *The Red and the Black,* gave it nothing like the response that it had had from my college generation. Then one day a whole class, almost all its members gifted men, agreed in saying that they were bored by Julien Sorel and didn't like him. Bored by Julien Sorel! But didn't he, I asked, represent their own desires for pre-eminence, their own natural young ambition? They snubbed me with their answer and fixed between themselves and me the great gulf of the generations: they did not, they said, understand ambition of Julien's self-referring kind; what they wanted was a decent, socially useful co-operative work to do. I felt like an aging Machiavelli among the massed secretariat of the U.N.

Young men of this kind certainly do not represent anything like the full development of the other-directed character which Mr. Riesman describes. It is even possible that their rejection of the extreme inner-direction of Julien Sorel is not so much in favor of other-direction as of the "autonomous" character which Mr. Riesman proposes as the possible optimum of our culture. More likely, however, they represent a compromise between inner-direction and other-direction. As such they make a spectacle which in many ways is very attractive.

But the tendency of other-direction does not stop with the character of these young men. And the consequences of its fuller development are disquieting. Mr. Riesman remarks that he has found it almost impossible to make a comparison of the two forms of character-direction without making inner-direction seem the more attractive of the two. I don't agree with Mr. Riesman that the preference is a mere prejudice which we must guard against. Granting all that is to be said against the tendency of inner-direction to cut itself off from what is warm and personal, granting too all that may be said for what other-direction does to refine leisure and consumption, it is still inner-direction that must seem the more fully human, even in its excess. Mr. Riesman himself seems to be saying something of this sort when, in speaking of the autonomous character, he remarks that the inner-directed character more closely resembles it than does the other-directed, and that, indeed, it is easier for inner-directed people to approach actual autonomy.

It is in any case true, on Mr. Riesman's showing, that the political life is far more likely to be healthy in a culture in which inner-direction is dominant. The exacerbated sense of others, of oneself in relation to others, does not, it seems, make for the sense of the polity. On the contrary—other-direction is concomitant with a sense of powerlessness in political matters, and this impotence masks itself in many ways, often as hatred of or contempt for politics. This in turn is easily rationalized into a desire for a meta-politics, for a perfect and absolute form of government which shall make impossible the conflict of wills of actual politics.

And the apathy which marks our political life lies as a threat beneath all the life of other-direction. Social approval and the desire for it are not love, nor even friendship, nor even community. The life of leisure, of fun, of narcissism, of right choice among the articles of consumption, of sex as the "last frontier" of adventure, of bland adjustment—this life is at every moment susceptible to the cankering boredom which lies beneath its surface.

This is not, I must make clear, the note on which Mr. Riesman ends. It is one of his decisive intellectual virtues that he has no love for the opiate of pessimism. He is not charmed by apocalyptic visions. It is not the end of a culture that he has undertaken to describe but a moment in its history.

1952

II

Although I had read most of the essays and studies that David Riesman had published in various journals over the past seven years and had admired them *seriatim,* I was not prepared for the effect they would make when marshalled in force and coherence in the volume called *Individualism Reconsidered.* It is a work that has all the cogency and originality of *The Lonely Crowd.* And because its energies are not subordinated to the necessities of developing a particular sociological thesis but are free to range over a wide variety of subjects, the new book is more vivacious and more personally immediate than its remarkable predecessor.

In writing about *The Lonely Crowd* I spoke of the jealousy of the social sciences which is likely to be felt by people of literary inclination—they are troubled because the social sciences seem to be expropriating literature from one of its most characteristic functions, the investigation of manners and morals. This jealousy I myself experienced intensely as I read *Individualism Reconsidered.* No American novel of recent years has been able to give me the sense of the actuality of our society that I get from Mr. Riesman's book, nor has any novel been able to suggest, as these essays so brilliantly do, the excitement of contemplating our life in culture as an opportunity and a danger.

It happened that I read Mr. Riesman's book just after I had gone through several recent novels of some pretension to social and moral seriousness. The authors of these books were known to me as men of good intellect and of a degree of talent which, if it is not of the highest, is certainly sufficient to do the job which we may reasonably expect will be done by the contemporary novel when we think of it in its wide generality and not merely as the high, fine product of a very few geniuses—the job, that is, of giving us reasonably accurate news of the world, of telling us the way things are. Only genius, of course, can tell us the way things *really* are; but there is a kind of information which falls short of this in accuracy and comprehensiveness and which is nevertheless interesting, and useful to have, and even necessary to have. But the novels I speak of told me only one thing about our life: that intelligent and serious men, such as these authors are, have the greatest difficulty nowadays in being even minimally aware of our life. And since the novelist's sense of the internal life is concomitant with his sense of external life, it seemed to me that these novelists were writing about people who did not exist, or who, if they did exist, might as well stop existing.

D. H. Lawrence called the novel "the book of life," and these novelists would have said no less in praise of the novel, and they were most touchingly devoted to life, and to "values," and to "affirmation," and to goodness in general—all of which had the effect of making me feel that I had been brushed by the wing of the Angel of Death. (No one has yet paid attention to the anti-catharsis, the generally anti-hygienic effect of bad serious art, the stimulation it gives to all one's neurotic tendencies, the literal, physically-felt depression it induces.)

But as I read Mr. Riesman I began again to believe that life was not merely a more troublesome form of death. There are no characters in his book, only situations, but I began to believe that people must really exist in order to create these situations, the reality of which cannot be doubted. And I could suppose that these people would some day present themselves in their actuality to some novelist who might not quite like them, who might even despair of them, but who would believe that they really existed, that they really made a society.

Mr. Riesman has the intrusive curiosity that is the mark of the classic novelist. The novelist, in his ideal character, is the artist who is consumed by the desire to know how things really are, who has entered into an elaborate romance with actuality. He is the artist of the conditioned, of the impingement of things upon spirit and of spirit upon things, and the success of his enterprise depends as much upon his awareness of things as upon his awareness of spirit. The intense concern with what Willa Cather contemptuously called the "furniture" of the novel is not peculiar to one school or tradition of novelists: it is endemic in the novel throughout its history, it is essential to the very idea of the novel. The fascinated preoccupation with the market for gold braid or the details of the paper trade with which we sometimes like to tease Balzac is not a mere neurotic compulsiveness or a gross naivety on the part of the great man—the fluctuations of the gold-braid market are the index of the fortunes of the Napoleonic spirit, the shift from linen-rag to cotton-rag in the making of paper is the direct effect of the triumph of the spirit of democracy. The sensitivity to things and the curiosity about them have been ineluctable for the novel from Cervantes to Proust and Joyce, even to Kafka.

In our fiction of the present time—the work of John O'Hara is an exception—this sensitivity and curiosity are less and less manifest. They seem to have taken refuge in sociology and cultural anthropology. In Mr. Riesman's work they prevail as the prime creative and controlling element of its intelligence. His mode of understanding begins with a question, and a real question, not a merely formal one. What actually is going on in our family life? in our modes of consumption? in our factories? in our board-rooms? in our schools? on the cinema screen? in the theater? in the courts? in the judge's chambers? in the political caucus? and in the political caucuses not only of majority parties but of marginal groups? And who but Mr. Riesman would give serious attention to the cultural implications of the social, ethnic, and intellectual characteristics of the editorial boards of student law reviews? Or consider at length the development of American football as the reflection of our social conditions and the expression of our social ideals? Or examine American Zionism objectively as a manifestation of elements of specifically American feeling?

In speaking of the diminution of literature's impulse to discover what is going on around us, we must have in mind not only our novelists but also our literary-intellectual class in its totality. So far as our culture generalizes itself and presents itself as an object for consideration and evaluation, it does so chiefly through the medium of our literary intellectuals. The virtues of this class are greater than people now seem to wish to admit, yet I think it is true to say of it that it seems to find more and more difficulty in believing that there is a significant reality to be found in anything except literature itself and a certain few moral assumptions which modern literature has made peculiarly its own; or in believing that any profession save that of literature is interesting and deserves credence. We live at a time when intellectual professions are proliferating as never before in history; we live at a time when ideas have become the very stuff of daily existence. Yet we really have no class of intellectuals who bring us the news of ideas. Mr. Riesman assumes a special place in our cultural life because he undertakes to tell us what is going on in the heads and hearts of city planners, and of sociologists, educationists, "recreationists"—it is news of the first importance that there are such people—and psychologists.

The sixth of the eight parts of Mr. Riesman's book is composed of four essays on Freud and psychoanalysis. The titles of the essays will in themselves suggest the cogency of Mr. Riesman's exposition of this subject: "The Themes of Work and Play in the Structure of Freud's Thought," "Authority and Liberty in the Structure of Freud's Thought," "The Themes of Heroism and Weakness in the Structure of Freud's Thought," "Freud, Religion and Science." With many of the things that Mr. Riesman says about Freud, there is much to be said in disagreement. But the essays are notable not only for their intrinsic intellectual interest but also for what they suggest about our intellectual life by their being virtually the unique consideration of Freud's ideas by a layman writing for laymen. Freud's effect upon our thought and feeling is, as Mr. Riesman says, incalculable. Yet most educated people still have but approximate notions of what Freud said, and I can think of no other occasion when he and his science have been the object of criticism as serious and systematic as Mr. Riesman's.

It has more than once been observed of the novelist that his relation to his society is an ambivalent one—he at once loves and hates the social world he lives in. He hates and despises and denounces his society and tries always to transcend it, but he cannot surrender his fascinated contemplation of it; he loves it if only for the occasion it provides for him to exercise his art of hating, despising, and denouncing. Almost, we might say, he cherishes it for giving him the opportunity for ambivalence, for being the Lesbia to whom he can say, Catullus-fashion, "Odi et amo"—there is, doubtless, a kind of pleasure of self-discovery, a pleasure of a personal-intellectual kind, in experiencing the balance of the two extreme emotions. And possibly we can account for the feebleness of the social intelligence which I have noted in the novels of our time by saying that it is the result of the resolution of the novelist's ambivalence, the suppression of one of its terms, or even both. He no longer says, "Odi et amo," scarcely even "Odi," and he has no desire to penetrate to society's fascinating, if fatal, secret. No novelist now would think of allegorizing society as Balzac did in the image of Foedora, a beautiful but heartless woman, *une belle dame sans merci*. Not only the novelist but a significant number of the mass of educated and articulate people have resolved, as it were, to withdraw both love and hate from society as a present actuality and to attach their hopes to some perfectly unambiguous social image of the past or future. In the course of his book Mr. Riesman several times touches upon this change in the attitude toward society, this growing tendency to regard with a sort of disengaged disgust the energies that are at work in the individualism of bourgeois, industrial, and urban society and fix the attention upon the "values of collective and folkish life," upon some "primitive" or "pastoral" ideal, as he calls it, an ideal which has been fortified by certain assumptions of a whole generation of cultural anthropologists.

Mr. Riesman himself finds it possible to maintain the old ambivalence toward society in full force, although in new form. He accepts society in all its paradoxes, ambiguities, anomalies, contradictions, and ironies. While believing that the only possible judgment of a given social fact is a personal-moral judgment, he never supposes that society and personal morality are identical and coextensive. He conceives society to be the field on which the conflicting claims of personal morality are worked out, or fought out under reasonably decent rules. And since these claims are complex, various, and sometimes irreconcilable, since the life of personality and morality cannot be made unitary, he believes that the ideal virtue of a society is a pragmatic virtue. He has, for example, no disposition to deplore the influence of bosses in city politics, for he conceives of the boss as a "broker" among the competing values of urban life, worth tolerating so long as he does his job adequately. He believes it to be a fallacy to "assume that people can co-operate only if they understand each other . . . or if they like each other, or if they share certain preconceptions." This being so, these elements of our society which have been traditionally regarded by articulate people of good will as objects of disgust, such as the market, or political parties that are not organized around ideologies and clearly formulated aims and ideals, appear to him as "social inventions" which, so far from being disgraceful, are actually the "glory" of a large-scale society tending toward democracy.

The pragmatic acceptance of society is morally possible, as Mr. Riesman of course knows, only under certain conditions. It needs an economic situation of at least relative prosperity, and it needs a society which actually is tending toward democracy, a society with a high degree of mobility making for an increasing equality. Such a situation, Mr. Riesman believes, prevails in America today, and it is producing what he makes bold to call "one of the great cultures of history." For this opinion, which is basic to all his thought about American society, Mr. Riesman has met resistance and even opprobrium from those people who feel it to be essential to their moral life to maintain an absolute and tragic conception of society against a pragmatic and ironic view. The opprobrium consists of leveling against Mr. Riesman the accusation of "conformity," of his having surrendered and submitted to the dominant values of American life which are known, by defiinition, to be bad. This is odd indeed when we·consider the intensity of Mr. Riesman's preoccupation with the virtues of nonconformity, and his concern with the strategies of resistance to dominant values.

For he is truly double-minded in his response to society—exactly in the degree that he accepts American society, he fears and suspects it. John Stuart Mill himself was not more apprehensive of the tyranny of the majority than Mr. Riesman is. For Mr. Riesman, as for Mill, the principle of individualism is morally prepotent and the freedom of the individual is the first criterion of social good.

Individual; individualism—the words have little charm for us these days, and Mr. Riesman ventures to recognize and challenge our apathy when he incorporates one of them, inert, ponderous, superannuated as it may seem, in the title of his lively and immediate book. Events have made the possibility of individualism a very narrow one, just as the pessimistic prophets had predicted. A long course of liberalistic thought, tinged with quasi-Marxism, has impressed upon us the virtues of "the group," of social-mindedness and cooperation, and has led us to feel that the word *individualism* is appropriate only to the cruder propaganda of business enterprise. It figures, too, we believe, as an all too appropriate element of the language of nations when they choose to affirm high ideals, or in the vocabulary of educationists when they feel they have perhaps said a little too much about "adjustment." Nowadays we are all deeply concerned about conformity, but it would be difficult to discover, in all the many denunciations of conformity that have been uttered, any conception or example of nonconformity that implies more than the holding of a particular set of political opinions—one sometimes feels that for many people the denunciation of McCarthyism constitutes their full imagination of how one may differentiate oneself from the dominant mass.

For Mr. Riesman, as for Mill, the freedom of the individual or of the minority or "marginal" group stands in perpetual danger of being encroached on by the majority. But where Mill was inclined to see the encroachment as political and overt, Mr. Riesman sees it as cultural and insidious, a distinction which defines the difference between the social thought of the nineteenth century and that of the twentieth. In contemporary American society the values of the majority are not imposed by coercion, as Mill feared they would be in nineteenth-century England, but, for the most part, simply by their being made available. The protection which was once afforded to sub-cultures by social distinction or by local isolation is no longer in force; and innumerable other social changes expose the individual and the minority group to the attraction and seduction of the dominant *mores,* with the result that even when a conscious effort is made to resist domination, it is likely to be made in terms that have been dictated by a majority. In one of his most interesting essays, Mr. Riesman suggests how Zionism and other forms of Jewish separatism are to be understood as manifestations of the American culture they are contrived to resist.

And where Mill conceived the strength of individualism to lie in the secure cohesiveness of the minority group, Mr. Riesman sees the danger to individualism that lies even in this seeming protection. He understands that the individual is threatened not only by the tyranny of the powerful but also by what he calls "the tyranny of the powerless . . . of beleaguered teachers, liberals, Negroes, women, Jews, intellectuals, and so on, over each other." Nothing is easier than for what he calls a "pet heresy" to become something like a popular orthodoxy, or at least "the vested heresy of an in-group." The social punishment meted out by the *cénacle* to the individual who questions its ideas is likely to be swifter and more direct than that of an affronted whole society.

With the possibility of tyranny omnipresent, with dominance become sly and bland, what help to individualism does Mr. Riesman give? In a way, his best help is implicit. It lies in his assumption of the pleasure of being an individual and free—in what we may call his "poetry" of individualism. The particular nature of this poetry of individualism must be specified, for in an age in which the conception of the individual is hard to maintain, we are likely to suppose that the only means of individualism are violent and absolute; the fierceness of, say, Rimbaud or Lawrence consorts with our notion of what it means to be an individual, but we have progressively dimmed our recollection of Montaigne. And perhaps the best way of suggesting the effect of Mr. Riesman's book is by reference to the poetry of individualism as it exists in Montaigne—to the stubbornness of Montaigne's sense of the self, to his privacy, to the catholicity of his awareness and responsiveness, to the virtues of his mind which he required to be, in the famous phrase, *ondoyant et divers*.

We have fallen into the habit of thinking of Montaigne's characteristic irony as negative. In point of fact, however, his relativism and his doubt are based on a faith of the most positive kind, an evaluation of the human soul transcending that of most Christian thinkers. Something of this faith is inherent in Mr. Riesman's thought and it accounts for and defines his own relativism and irony. It is what leads him to his own way of being *ondoyant et divers*, modulating his doctrine according to the nature of his audience, taking it to be his intellectual duty to guard against confirming any group in its righteousness or self-pity or in the orthodoxy of its heresy. It leads him to conceive the right relation of the individual to society to be that of "conditional co-operation" in specific, short-term enterprises, rather than an absolute or total commitment. It leads him to defend any group that raises a question in society, or that preserves any particular high standard, or that exemplifies any special intellectual or moral virtue, even if the existence of its admirable qualities entails qualities that are not admirable.

And it is this faith that makes it possible for him to assert what in our day will seem a difficult idea even to people of great moral sensitivity—that one may live a real life apart from the group, that one may exist as an actual person not only at the center of society but on its margins, that one's values may be none the less real and valuable because they do not prevail and are even rejected and submerged, that as a person one has not ceased to exist because one has "failed." That this needs to be said suggests the peculiar threat to the individual that our society offers. That Mr. Riesman says it as cogently and movingly as he does will suggest the importance of his book.

1954

Dr. Leavis and
the Moral Tradition

IN THE course of his book on the English novel, *The Great Tradition*, F. R. Leavis finds occasion to deal with certain remarks of Lord David Cecil, and perhaps nothing could more immediately suggest Dr. Leavis's quality as a critic than his part in this brief transaction. Lord David is going about the familiar business of explaining the Puritan nature of George Eliot's morality, and in the familiar vein:

She might not believe in heaven and hell and miracles, but she believed in right and wrong, and man's paramount obligation to follow right, as strictly as if she were Bunyan himself. And her standards of right and wrong were the Puritan standards. She admired truthfulness and chastity and industry and self-restraint, she disapproved of loose living and recklessness and deceit and self-indulgence.

And Dr. Leavis responds:

I had better confess that I differ (apparently) from Lord David Cecil in sharing these beliefs, admirations, and disapprovals, so that the reader knows my bias at once. And they seem to me favourable to the production of great literature. I will add (exposing myself completely) that the enlightenment of aestheticism or sophistication that feels an amused superiority to them leads, in my view, to triviality and boredom, and that out of triviality comes evil.

Here, in its forthrightness and downrightness—and rightness—we have Dr. Leavis's moral feeling, which is everywhere to be found as a shaping and strengthening element in his criticism. And here, too, we have the energy of his protestantism, which has made him so notable and stormy a figure in English letters—a man of disciples and enemies, the teacher who has made the relatively new and obscure Downing College a dissident center of English studies at Cambridge, training the students who have devotedly carried his ideas to the secondary schools and provincial universities of Britain; the educational reformer who has made a frontal attack on the academic methods of literary instruction; the editor who, in his quarterly review, *Scrutiny,* has fostered a critical movement of considerable power at the same time that he himself has developed into one of the most formidable of modern critics.

Dr. Leavis is not a critic who works by elaborated theory. As between Coleridge, on the one hand, and Dr. Johnson and Matthew Arnold, on the other, he has declared his strong preference for the two latter—for the critic, that is, who requires no formulated first principles for his judgment but only the sensibility that is the whole response of his whole being. Dr. Leavis's own critical sensibility is characteristically a moral one, not only in the sense that he happily affirms the value of common morality but also in the sense that, having perceived life to be of a certain weight and pressure, he requires of art that it react to experience with a proportionate counterthrust of commitment, endurance, and intelligence. "A vital capacity for experience, a kind of reverent openness before life, and a marked moral intensity" are the particular criteria by which he judges the novel and by which he selects the five novelists who constitute for him what he calls the great tradition of the novel in England— George Eliot, Henry James, and Joseph Conrad, whom he discusses at length, and Jane Austen and D. H. Lawrence, whom he treats in passing.

The list, imposing as it is, will surprise many by its exclusiveness. This surprise, and the dissent that goes with it, Dr. Leavis is willing to incur. He does not mean to say that there are no other novelists in English worth reading, but he does intend to establish a critical line for purposes of discrimination in the field of fiction, a field that, as he rightly says, "offers such insidious temptations to complacent confusions of judgment and to critical indolence." He has done one of the most useful jobs that the critic can do—he has constituted a coherent tradition and has thus made a large body of work the more easily available to understanding. And it is true that, as he suggests, the particular tradition which he isolated is the one that is most communicable to the practitioner of the novel today; if we add Tolstoy and Dostoievski to the English list, we have the masters of the novel from whom most may at this moment be learned. Then, too, I feel sure, any discussion of the form of the novel that is likely to be meaningful must accept the strong emphasis Dr. Leavis puts upon "marked moral intensity," for it is upon the degree and quality of moral intensity that all aesthetic considerations of the novel depend. After all the nonsense that has been uttered about the technique of the novel, and especially after all the preciosity that has been offered in tribute to Jane Austen, what a relief it is to have Dr. Leavis give us this:

When we examine the formal perfection of *Emma,* we find that it can be appreciated only in terms of the moral preoccupations that characterize the novelist's peculiar interest in life. Those who suppose it to be an "aesthetic matter," a beauty of "composition" that is combined, miraculously, with "truth to life," can give no adequate reason for the view that *Emma* is a great novel, and no intelligent account of its perfection of form.

What a relief, too, to come on the other results of Dr. Leavis's critical intelligence—the vigor of his discrimination among James's novels, which is so useful whether or not one agrees with it; his cutting through the old prejudices about George Eliot to perceive her greatness; his dismissal of the trifling denigrations of Lawrence, which nowadays are offered with such a mechanical solicitude for artistic and political purity, and his perception of Lawrence's achievement as "a technical inventor, an innovator, a master of language"; his cool certainty, in the face of much authoritative opinion to the contrary, that Djuna Barnes's *Nightwood* is without value, that

Virginia Woolf's art is minor, that *Moll Flanders* is not a great novel, that *Hard Times is* a great novel. This is critical judgment of the first order, and its force and accuracy come in large part from Dr. Leavis's moral directness.

But the mention of *Hard Times* brings us up short and suggests that there are occasions when the relation between Dr. Leavis's intelligence and his moral sense is not maintained. *Hard Times* is the only one of Dickens's novels that Dr. Leavis admits to the great tradition. Were Dr. Leavis establishing not *the* great tradition but *a* great tradition, or if, using an acceptable meaning of the word, he had undertaken to discern the *classic* tradition, we would have no cause to question him. But this is not Dr. Leavis's way of doing things; he is nothing if not positive. He truly admires the genius of Dickens, but he excludes him from the great tradition. The reason he gives is that "the adult mind doesn't as a rule find in Dickens a challenge to an unusual and sustained seriousness." If we then ask why *Hard Times* does issue the challenge and the others of Dickens's novels do not, we see that it is because *Hard Times* drives directly and unremittingly at its point of moral attack—upon the culture of utilitarianism—and does not stop on its way to create those masses of what Dr. Leavis calls "irrelevant 'life'" that characterize the other novels and make Dickens, for Dr. Leavis, primarily an entertainer and the best possible author for children.

Behind this judgment lies an assumption that is of the very greatest importance in Dr. Leavis's critical view. It is the same assumption that is at work when Dr. Leavis, in praising the wit of George Eliot's dialogue, compares it to Congreve's and then goes on to say that it is superior to Congreve's because it does not offer us "wit and phrasing for our admiration and the delight of our palates," or when he dismisses the author of *Tristram Shandy* with a reference to "irresponsible (and nasty) trifling," or when he suggests that *The Egoist* has no value at all. "Critics have found me narrow," says Dr. Leavis, yet it isn't a lack of catholicity that one objects to here but a basic error about the nature of art—and of life. For Dr. Leavis is saying in effect that art has its true being only in tension and direction, only in completely organized consciousness and moral clarity. He takes no proper account, that is, of the art that delights—and enlightens—by the intentional relaxation of moral awareness, by its invitation to us to contemplate the mere excess of irrelevant life. Nor does he take any account of the impulse of sheer *performance,* even of virtuosity, which, whether we respond to it in acrobatics or in athletics or in prestidigitation or in the ballet or in music or in literature, is of enormous human significance. Ultimately, indeed, both these elements of art have great moral relevance, which is why the critic must make his discriminations among them, not turn from them as if they were aberrations from maturity. "Awareness of the possibilities of life" is a quality that Dr. Leavis attributes to the major novelists, and marked moral intensity does of course contribute to the awareness of the possibilities of life. But so does the mind's delight in itself, in its power of excess and fantasy, in its ability to play the game of freedom, even freedom from law and the moral order, in its dream that, as Yeats said, life might overflow "without ambitious pains" and that it might "choose whatever shape it wills."

If we ask why a critic of Dr. Leavis's powers makes so little of the excessive or free or virtuose qualities of art, the answer seems to be that he has identified these qualities of art with a social group which appears to claim these qualities as characterizing its manner of life, a social group to which Dr. Leavis is antagonistic. One cannot but see that, in his reply to Lord David Cecil, Dr. Leavis is implying a comparison not only of two moral ideals but of two social ideals as well. Sooner or later, of course, any critic of large mind will touch upon social matters, because what we call culture may be defined as the locus of the meeting of literature with social actions and attitudes. English literary life is marked by certain social features to which we in this country have no precise counterpart and which are likely to bring the critic to a consideration of social matters more immediately than with us. Thus, although now and then the word "aristocratic" is used by us as a term of praise or blame, it is known to be just a way of speaking. But in England a definite social value does attach to a good many literary people, as, for example, the Bloomsbury group, of which, if one says that it is aristocratic, one uses the word not with literal accuracy (the group being predominantly of the upper-middle class) but at least with some meaning, for in the legend of its manner of life, as well as in its literary style, the qualities of freedom and virtuosity, in the form of elegance and felicity, are predominant. A retrospective glance over *Scrutiny* will suggest that although Dr. Leavis and his coadjutors are strict with anyone who does not meet their high demands for literature, they take an especial pleasure in being strict with Bloomsbury. The same preference of attack marks *The Great Tradition*—it is not merely the accepted wrong ideas about literature that Dr. Leavis seeks to scotch but the ideas of a privileged class represented by such writers as Lord David Cecil, Lytton Strachey, Clive Bell, and Virginia Woolf. The Cromwellian revolution never really came to an end in England, and we can say of Dr. Leavis that he has organized the lofty intellectual expression of its late, endemic form. With this, one can easily be sympathetic—there is reasonable cause for impatience with the ideal of life that is suggested by Clive Bell or Lytton Strachey or Virginia Woolf. Yet it is a matter for wonder that a critical movement of the power of the *Scrutiny* group should have been drawn to social considerations no larger than this; one has the impression that it conceives all the world's issues as existing between its ideal readers, who are persons "seriously interested in literature," and a lesser breed of mere triflers. In Dr. Leavis's own critical practice, the failure to be explicit about even the disproportionately small social issue of Bloomsbury has led to his assimilating a social antagonism into his general critical sensibility, where it works to distort his perception of an important aspect of literature. For one feels that it is not the actual qualities of Congreve, Sterne, Dickens, and Meredith that Dr. Leavis is responding to when he dismisses them but rather the simulacra of these qualities as they have been used in, say, Virginia Woolf's *Orlando* and as they there suggest the social qualities he dislikes.

No doubt this constitutes a sizable fault in Dr. Leavis's criticism, and yet it is by no means a decisive fault. It isn't by his freedom from error that we properly judge a critic's value but by the integrity and point of his whole critical impulse, which, if it is personal and committed in the demands it makes upon life and literature, will be as instructive in its errors as in its correct judgments. It is possible to disagree with half the critical statements Dr. Leavis may make and yet know him to be a critic of the first importance.

1949

Profession: Man of the World

I

THE addicted reader of Victorian memoirs and biographies knows them to be haunted by a presence which appears sometimes as "Mr. Monckton Milnes (now Lord Houghton)," and sometimes as "Lord Houghton (then Mr. Monckton Milnes)." To our dim sight this ubiquitous being seems to have accomplished only one thing in his lifetime that makes him worthy of recollection—he wrote a biography of Keats before anyone quite knew who Keats was. But we naturally assume that this work has been superseded, that modern scholarship has made it as ghostly as its author, and we rest content with this knowledge of Monckton Milnes: that he spent his life knowing everyone who was likely to make an item in any biographical dictionary, that he introduced everyone to everyone else at his breakfast parties, his dinner parties, his house parties.

If we look a little more particularly into the circumstances of his life, we find Milnes to have been a dilettante poet who achieved a considerable reputation for his sentimental verse but who had no great opinion of his powers in poetry and sensibly gave it up at forty. (He is, however, to be remembered as the author of the nursery classic "Lady Moon, Lady Moon.") He was an ambitious but quite unsuccessful political personage during his many years in the House of Commons, an inveterate traveler, a notorious gossip, something of a wit, something of a glutton—"My exit," he said, "will be the result of too many entrées."

Of the innumerable contemporary references that are made to Monckton Milnes, not a few are of a condescending sort. Disraeli despised him and left an extensive memorandum of his low opinion of Milnes; and Milnes, having had the foolhardiness to reproach Disraeli for not having included him among the characters to be recognized in *Coningsby,* found himself depicted as the Mr. Vavasour of *Tancred,* a satirical portrait which is not as destructive as it was intended to be, for Disraeli, noting the flibbertigibbet quality of Milnes, his love of celebrated people and his social busyness, could yet not bring himself to conceal his subject's genuine sweetness and powers of sympathy, or even the charm of the gusto with which he pursued his social enterprises. The point of condescension, when it was expressed, was that Milnes was a fribble. He was known to have talent, and it was believed that he had sacrificed it to vanity. His wit was not of a malicious kind and so it was not feared; it was therefore despised, as was his pleasure in talk and his insatiable social curiosity.

Sometimes the references to Milnes are charged with moral disapproval. The collections of his notable library were devoted to several interesting subjects, of which one was erotica; he had a particular interest in the works of the Marquis de Sade, who at that time was not the respectable philosophical figure he has since become, a sort of erogenous Spinoza. Swinburne browsed through this collection with delight, and it helped him to realize and encouraged him to express his already developed perversity. The French biographer of Swinburne, Georges Lafourcade, and the Italian chronicler of Romantic sadism, Mario Praz, have therefore represented Lord Houghton (formerly Mr. Monckton Milnes) as a sinister figure, one of those Milords whose devotion to the whip and the birch was understood on the Continent to be a characteristic trait of the English aristocracy, and they have written of Fryston, his country house, as a seat of iniquity.

The moral condemnation can be dismissed—the interest of Milnes in Sadic erotica was apparently not much more perverse than that of any of my readers whose eye has quickened at the sight of the phrase; and Milnes did nothing to corrupt Swinburne and much to help him.

As for the tone of condescension, this must be accepted as an essential part of the legend of Monckton Milnes. It is what gives a special meaning to the affection which many people felt for him and to the admiration for him which they expressed in language of a peculiar eloquence. It must surely have been a very rare kind of social butterfly that could have won from Carlyle the particular grace and simplicity of love and respect which he gave to Dickie Milnes. Someone once said that Lord Houghton was a good man to go to in trouble, and W. E. Forster, Matthew Arnold's brother-in-law, a Quaker of considerable austerity, capped this praise by saying in reply, "Yes, but more than that, he is a good man to go to in disgrace." People of high principle and fine sensitivity were moved to speak of him with a curious profundity of feeling, as if they saw his extravagant sociability, his mildly snobbish aspirations, his gossip, his self-indulgence, not merely as the mask of a peculiar benevolence but as in some way its natural ground. It is as if, when they tried to praise him, they were confronted with a new possibility of human nature. They seem to have felt a gush of astonishment and relief that goodness should come out of "the world" and out of worldliness, that virtue should be of the world worldly.

In middle life Milnes thought he ought to marry, and he did marry, very suitably and happily. But before he met the lady who was to be his wife, he was drawn to a strange and very charming young woman who was, of all women, Florence Nightingale. He proposed marriage and was gently rejected. This seems expectable enough, considering the enormous disparity between the two temperaments; what we do not expect is that Florence Nightingale should have recorded in her diary how deeply involved with Milnes she felt herself to be, and her indications that she did not quite forgive him for having accepted his *congé* so easily. After his death she wrote of him to his sister:

He had the same voice and manner for a dirty brat as for a duchess—the same desire to give pleasure and good. . . . He had I believe the genius of friendship in philanthropy—not philanthropy—but treating *all* his fellow mortals as if they were his brothers and sisters.

For Americans it is Henry Adams's estimate of Milnes that is likely to be the most memorable and telling. One of the remarkable things about Milnes was that at a time when London society was being as intensely anti-American as if it had been reading *The New Statesman* of our present day and made a point of being openly rude to American visitors, Milnes was firm in his pro-American feelings. It was to him that all distinguished Americans came, and he introduced them to his wide circle, and saw to it that they saw what they wanted to see. When the Civil War broke out and British society sided solidly with the South and discovered that there really were American gentlemen after all, Milnes stood fast in his Northern sympathies. Henry Adams, remembering the first dark days of his father's ministry to England, kept fresh Milnes's great kindness to him. At the Fryston house party to which Milnes invited him, he not only had his first tremendous sight of Swinburne, the first poet he had ever seen, but also his first experience of the pleasure of *talk*. Of Milnes, Adams wrote in the *Education:*

Monckton Milnes was a social power in London, possibly greater than Londoners themselves quite understood, for in London Society as elsewhere, the dull and ignorant made a majority, and dull men always laughed at Monckton Milnes. . . . He himself affected social eccentricity, challenging ridicule with the indifference of one who knew himself to be the first wit in London and a maker of men—of a great many men. A word from him went far. An invitation to his breakfast table went farther. Behind his almost Falstaffian mask and laugh of Silenus, he carried a fine, broad and high intelligence which no one questioned. As a young man he had written verses which some readers thought poetry and which were certainly not altogether prose. Later in Parliament he made speeches chiefly criticized as too good for the place and too high for the audience.

Socially, he was one of the two or three men who went everywhere, knew everybody, talked of everything and had the ear of Ministers. . . . He was a voracious reader, a strong critic, an art connoisseur in certain directions, but above all he was a man of the world by profession and loved the contacts—and perhaps the collisions—of society. Milnes was the good nature of London; the Gargantuan type of its refinement and coarseness; the most universal figure of Mayfair.

II

Richard Monckton Milnes was the son of a country gentleman, Robert Pemberton Milnes, who was descended from a manufacturing family; his mother was a daughter of Lord Galway, a notorious drunkard. The elder Milnes was a man sufficiently remarkable in himself. He had greater natural force than his son, and the son was a disappointment to the father. Richard Monckton Milnes was able to win influence, but not power. Henry Adams is right in saying he had the ear of Ministers; but he had it only in certain matters—when it came to a question of a literary pension or a post in the British Museum or an Abbey burial, Milnes could get his way, but he had no credit in weightier matters. He was not a strong man in debate; but beyond that, all the Prime Ministers in his lifetime seem to have known by their animal faculty of apperception that he was not the sort of man to whom power is given—Prime Ministers know such things by sniffing. But so strong had been his father's political scent that in 1809, at the age of twenty-six, Pemberton Milnes was offered a seat in the Cabinet, either as Chancellor of the Exchequer or Secretary of War. But he said, "Oh, no. I will not accept either. With my temperament I should be dead in a year." He did not specify what element of his temperament would have made his acceptance fatal. His wife begged him on her knees to reconsider (for the sake of the children), but he would not, and retired to the country as a private gentleman.

"My father," Monckton Milnes wrote in his commonplace-book,

"was always trying to give me two educations at once, one an education of ambition, vanity, emulation and progress . . . the other of independence, self-abnegation and the highest repose. He thus failed in making me either a successful politician or a contented philosopher." The relation between the father and the son was affectionate but antagonistic, and touched with a rather wry comedy. Pemberton Milnes was a Tory; his son, as he matured, took the liberal, and on the whole the intelligent, side of every public question, and he disliked country sports. The father was of the eighteenth century, and he thought the son soft, especially in his prose style, and commented frequently on his looseness of diction. He was outraged that Richard should use the phrase "balance the plain reasonableness"—"You balance probabilities—not reasonableness." And why should reasonableness be called *plain* reasonableness? Again: "p. 18—*sodden* ruins—what are *sodden* ruins?" The comedy of the relationship reached its high point when the son managed to snag a peerage for his aged father, which, of course, he looked to inherit, and the father coolly replied to the Prime Minister that on grounds of principle he could not accept what had been offered.

In 1823 Monckton Milnes went to Trinity College, Cambridge, where his talent and charm soon involved him in that world of sentimental and more-or-less erotic friendship which marked the life of the upper-class young Englishman at school and college, of which the relationship of Tennyson and Hallam is the best-known instance. Milnes, indeed, was a member of the famous "Apostles" group of Tennyson and Hallam. "That is a man I should like to know," Tennyson said to himself when, entering Trinity for the first time, he passed Milnes: "he looks like the best-tempered fellow in the world." Between Tennyson and Milnes there was a long and comfortable regard. Hallam was less responsive and there is an interesting letter in which Hallam says that he can give Milnes sympathy but not friendship in the true, high sense of that sacred word.

After leaving Trinity, Milnes went for a time to the university at Bonn, and there began his knowledge and love of German literature.

His family having taken up residence in Italy, he spent a considerable time with them and then went on a tour of Greece, which was at that time a sufficiently venturesome enterprise. He made friends wherever he went, seeming to suppose that it was his clear business in life to know whoever was distinguished and interesting. His Boswellian acquisitiveness went with a tendency to a Boswellian failure of tact, and the report he received of his extended visit to Scotland indicated that he had left behind him a long trail of offense. He could make dreadful *gaffes* even in later life, when his social experience was enormous, as witness the awful dinner he gave in Paris, which appalled his friend Tocqueville and offended Prosper Mérimée. Tocqueville thought the company *"fort peu homogène"*—so badly assorted, indeed, as to constitute either a scandalous lapse of taste or a bad joke; Mérimée could not understand why, among the lesser social discomforts of the evening, he had been required to confront George Sand, whom he loathed after his brief affair with her.

The same failure of tact that could now and then overtake Milnes in his social life—it was a sort of blundering innocence—marks his whole life as a political figure. He entered the House of Commons as a member from Pontrefact, of which his father had become the squire, and he seems to have blundered at every turn. He was by no means stupid *about* politics, only *in* politics. He might have made a perfectly good political historian, but he was not meant for caucuses and committees. His political life was all bitterness to him, yet he loved it, and he could not imagine giving up his membership in the "best club in London." Social life became his chief interest, but we do not understand what Milnes felt about social life if we do not see that the only society that could interest him was one in which power of some kind, either intellectual or political, was to be seen at its work.

It is at this point that we must speak of the excellence of Mr. Pope-Hennessy's biography of Milnes. Mr. Pope-Hennessy has clearly perceived that the first virtue of the biography of such a man as

Monckton Milnes is a quantitative virtue. The mass of detail of which Milnes's life was made up is of its very essence. A great novelist—Henry James, of course—might have conveyed the moral interest of Monckton Milnes's life, that of the worldling endowed with an unlooked-for moral grace which depends for its existence upon the very worldliness that makes its existence surprising. But we should always be called upon to substantiate the ideas from the good will of our imaginations; we should have been deprived of the pleasure of having the unlikely truth *demonstrated* to us, of having the moral interest unfolded in slow, uneconomical specificity, in friendship after friendship, party after party, journey after journey, vanity after vanity, benevolence after benevolence. In the management of detail Mr. Pope-Hennessy cannot be bettered. No event or circumstance is too small for him to note, no character whose path crosses Milnes's is too obscure for him to portray. At first we may wonder what we have let ourselves in for in the way of heaped-up minutiae, but very soon, as Mr. Pope-Hennessy proceeds at his equable, leisurely pace, the peculiar aesthetic of detail asserts itself. And, aesthetics apart, we begin to understand how rich a perception of an era and a society we are being given. The two volumes of Mr. Pope-Hennessy's life make a conspectus of the intellectual and social life of the nineteenth century which is not surpassed in fullness and liveliness by any other work I can call to mind.*

---

* There are one or two objections to be made of a minor, or carping, kind. I do not know who it was who instructed the English writers of nineteenth-century biographies that Wordsworth is the very type of sentimentality and taught them that whenever they refer to sentimentality they should call it "Wordsworthian sentimentality." Mr. Pope-Hennessy has not freed himself of this bad practice. Then one could wish (especially since Sir Edward Marsh is thanked for his advice on style) that Mr. Pope-Hennessy had not exemplified the tendency of English writers to follow us Americans in the use of certain slovenly neologisms. The verb *enthuse*, a "back-formation" from *enthusiasm* which implies ignorance of the meaning of the original word, ought not to be used by a thoughtful writer. Nor should a nineteenth-century character (or anybody) be spoken of as "getting his personality across." Then on two pages (34 and 35 of the second volume) Mr. Pope-Hennessy falls prey to a sort of buck-fever as he undertakes to deal with an American aspect of his subject. He begins by telling us that a certain Mrs. Twistleton had been born Ellen Dwight, "the daughter of a member for the Province of Massachusetts in the House of Representatives." The best opinion holds that by the nineteenth century Massachusetts was al-

A gifted young woman, Julia Wedgwood, who knew Milnes when he was getting on in years, said this of him:

I have a weakness for Lord Houghton; there seems to me something manqué about him, which always draws me toward people. I think in those odd omnium gatherum collections of his there is such a curious kind of aspiration after excellence in one walk or another, and then he is content to be 2nd rate himself, which very few people are.

There is a kind of wry delicacy in this characterization of Milnes, and it really does constitute a tribute. Yet it misses the one quality of Milnes that makes it wrong for anyone to condescend to him, however affectionately. That quality is his intelligence. Milnes was a man of high, if not intense, intelligence. It required intelligence—not merely taste—and it required the courage of intelligence to value Keats when Keats's admirers could be counted on the fingers of one's hands and when he was thought of, by those who knew him at all, as a corrupt sensualist; and to value Blake when scarcely anyone else did; and to see Tocqueville's genius at first glimpse; and to be the friend of Heine and Bettina von Arnim. We jib, of course, at Milnes's friendship with Louis Napoleon, and royal princesses, and queens, at his happiness in attending openings and inaugurations and official junkets. But none of his liking for the official and the grand ever qualified his feeling for the personal, the talented, the unsuccessful. In the help of men of letters that he either extorted from the government or gave himself, he constitutes a kind of fore-

---

ready what in this country we call a Commonwealth. Then, going on to speak of Hawthorne, Mr. Pope-Hennessy refers to him as the author of a work called *The House With the Seven Gables*, which is not unlike referring to *The Mill Upon the Floss*, or *A Tale About Two Cities*, or *Much Ado Concerning Nothing*. Having mentioned Hawthorne as the author also of *The Scarlet Letter* and *The Blithedale Romance*, he tells us that "his name more happily survives" by the *Tanglewood Tales*, which is as if he had said that Dickens's name is most happily kept in memory by *A Child's History of England*. Having occasion to refer to *The English Notebooks of Hawthorne*, he speaks of them as having been "very sanely edited" by Professor Randall Stewart, as if the *Notebooks* were a natural temptation to editorial frenzy, an impression which he confirms by speaking of them as having been "sponsored" in England by the Oxford University Press; in my experience, the O.U.P. publishes rather than sponsors books, and I cannot understand why it should have changed its practice on this one occasion.

runner of the modern Foundation, except that he had three qualities that no Foundation is likely to have in relation to literature—courage, intelligence, and sincerity.

How very widely assorted were the traits that make up Milnes's curious personal distinction and how simply and frankly his biographer has confronted them may be suggested by the characteristics of Milnes which are listed in the admirable index to the first of Mr. Pope-Hennessy's volumes. They make an irresistible human being:

Ambition
Beauty, quick response to
Boisterous high spirits
Charm of personality
Contrariness
Disinterestedness
Easy manner
Eccentricity and love of sensation
Emotionalism
Enthusiasm, capacity for
Flippancy
Friendship, genius for
Gaiety
Generosity
Genius, affinity to
Good nature and easy-going
   temperament
Good temper
Gossip, love of
Hospitable instincts
Humour, sense of
Imagination
Indolence

Kindheartedness and sympathetic helpfulness
Liberalism of mind
Magpie mind
Moodiness
Music, boredom with
Nervousness as a speaker
Notoriety, passion for
Open-mindedness
Originality of mind
Paradox, love of
Passionate love, incapacity for
Persistence
Pessimism
Pomposity in public speaking
Radicalism in literary judgment
Restlessness
Romanticism
Self-confidence
Sensitiveness and vulnerability
Sensuality
Sociability
Tact

Tactlessness
Tolerance
Touchiness
Toughness
Urbanism

Vivacity
Volatility
Volubility
Wit

1955

Adams at Ease

I T IS impossible to be consistent in the feelings with which we respond to Henry Adams. Sometimes he is irresistible, as in his memories of his boyhood, or in the exercise or expression of friendship, or in some fleeting reference to his dead wife. Sometimes he is hateful, as in his anti-Jewish utterances, or in the queer malice with which he infused the visions of doom of his later life. There are times when he is supreme in manly delicacy, and times when he seems feline, or trifling and shallow. It often occurs to us to believe that his is the finest American intelligence we can possibly know, while again it sometimes seems that his mind is so special, and so refined in specialness, as to be beside any possible point.

It would of course be easier for us to settle our personal accounts with him if only his personality were a private one. We might then choose simply to conclude that the flaws of his temper are of a kind that prevents us from giving him full credence. Or we might feel, with more charity and worldliness, that this was a man who lived to be eighty years old, who was articulate for more than sixty of those years, and who, one way or another, made himself the subject of all that he said, who, although not a confessional writer as we nowadays understand that term, was not bound by conventions of reticence other than those he created for himself—we might well feel of such a man that it would be strange indeed if he did not exhibit a good many of the inadequacies that the human spirit is heir to.

But it is not easy to come to a final settlement with Adams's personality either in the way of condemnation or in the way of tolerance because, as I say, it isn't a private personality that we are dealing with: it is a public issue. And it is not an issue that in the course of our lifetime we are likely to take a fixed position on. Once we involve ourselves with Adams, we are fated to be back and forth with him, now on one side of the issue, now on the other, as the necessities of our mood and circumstance dictate. We are at one with Adams whenever our sense of the American loneliness and isolation becomes especially strong, whenever we feel that our culture belongs to everyone except ourselves and our friends, whenever we believe that our talents and our devotion are not being sufficiently used. At such moments we have scarcely any fault to find with Adams the man. His temperamental failings sink out of sight beneath his large and noble significance.

Yet it isn't possible to identify ourselves with Adams for very long. One's parsnips must be already buttered, as Adams's were, before one can despair as wholeheartedly as he. One needs what he had, a certain elegance of *décor,* something of an almost princely style of life, a close and intimate view of the actuality of the power one undertakes to despise, and freedom to travel and observe, and leisure to pursue the studies by which one fleshes the anatomy of one's dark beliefs. And even apart from the economic considerations, we can't long afford the identification with Adams. We come to see, as William James saw, that there is a kind of corruption and corruptingness in the perfect plenitude of his despair. With James we understand that Adams's despair is a chief condition of its own existence, and that the right to hope is earned by our courage in hoping. And when we see this, we turn on Adams, using against him every weapon on which we can lay our hands. We look for the weaknesses in his theory of history and of society (it is not hard to find them), we question his understanding of science, we seek out the rifts in his logic—and we insist, of course, on the faults of his personal temper, we permit his irony to irritate us, we call him snobbish, and over-fastidious, and *fainéant.*

But we shall be wrong, we shall do ourselves a great disservice, if ever we try to read Adams permanently out of our intellectual life. I have called him an issue—he is even more than that, he is an indispensable element of our thought, he is an instrument of our intelligence. To succeed in getting rid of Adams would be to diminish materially the seriousness of our thought. In the intellectual life there ought to be frequent occasions for the exercise of ambivalence, and nothing can be more salutary for the American intelligence than to remain aware of Adams and to maintain toward him a strict ambivalence, to weigh our admiration and affection for him against our impatience and suspicion.

Two recent Adams items seem to me peculiarly useful in helping us keep the right balance of our emotions toward their author. Newton Arvin has made a selection of Adams's letters in the Great Letters Series, the publishers of which, Farrar, Straus and Young, have met the occasion of the presidential convention season with a new printing of Adams's Washington novel, *Democracy*. If, as I think, the scales have tipped rather against Adams in the last few years—is this because some of his worst predictions have come dismally true?—if at the moment he is more out of favor than in, these two books will do much to restore the equipoise of our judgment.

Adams, as we all remember, thought of himself as a child of the eighteenth century, and his belief in his anachronism is substantiated by nothing so much as his letters. His family was formidable in the epistolary art, his grandmother Abigail being something of a genius in it, and Henry practiced it with an appropriate seriousness. Early in his career he speaks half-jokingly of a desire to emulate Horace Walpole in the representation of the manners and habits of his time, and he made bold to hope that his letters would be remembered when much in the historical scene was forgotten. There is a common belief that those who write letters to posterity as well as to their friends are bound to write dully, but this is not true in general and it certainly is not true of Adams. Since personal letters were first valued and published, no public or quasi-public person can write them without the awareness of posterity. And of course for Adams archives were no great thing, and the notion that he was adding to their number did not make him awkward or, in the bad sense, self-conscious. The historical past, the historical present, the historical future, were the stuff of his existence, the accepted circumstance of his most private thoughts and most intimate friendships.

Adams's capacity for friendship was one of the most notable things about him, and it is of course a decisive element of the greatness of his letters. In this he is peculiarly a man of the nineteenth century, which was the great age of friendship. Men then felt that the sharing of experience with certain chosen spirits was one of the essential pleasures of life, and even writers and revolutionaries found it possible to have close, continuing communication with each other. Adams, we almost come to believe as we read his letters, was the last man, or perhaps the last American, to have had actual friendships. He mistrusted much in the world, but he trusted his friends, and he so far developed his great civilized talent for connection that he could be in lively communicative relationship even with his family, and even with women.

Mr. Arvin has selected the letters with his usual tact and perceptiveness, and with the awareness of how much they add to, and deduct from, and in general qualify the image of Adams's mind which we get from his two most famous books, *Mont-Saint-Michel and Chartres* and *The Education*. In the letters it was possible for Adams's mind to work without the excessive elaborations of irony which are characteristic of his published late writings. This irony is no doubt always very brilliant, but as Mr. Arvin observes, it is all too obviously less a function of the author's intelligence than of his personal uneasiness in relation to the unknown reader, of that excess of delicacy and self-regard which led him into the irritating highjinks of flirtatious hesitation about publishing his two great works. But in the letters there is no embarrassment and there is no irony beyond what normally and naturally goes with the exercise of a complex intelligence.

Then the letters, as Mr. Arvin remarks, give us an Adams who loved the world in its manifold variety much more than we might ever conclude from the books. He delighted in the pleasures that the world could offer, in what might be observed of the world for the joy of observation rather than for the support of a theory of the world's uninhabitability. Further, it is from the letters that we get a notion of the development of Adams's mind which is more accurate than his own formal account of it in *The Education*. "Only the reader of the letters," as Mr. Arvin says, "has a full sense of the delicacy with which Adams's mind was for many years balanced between the poles of hopefulness and despair, affirmation and denial, belief and skepticism."

Certainly the reader of the letters gets what the reader of *The Education* does not get, the awareness of how late in coming was Adams's disillusionment with democracy. *The Degradation of the Democratic Dogma* was not the title that Adams himself gave to the oddly contrived posthumous volume that his brother edited and published under that name, but it is a phrase that accurately suggests Adams's attitude in his last years, and *The Education* would lead us to believe that this attitude was established with him upon the defeat of his youthful political expectations with the publication of the list of Grant's Cabinet. Yet the letters of the middle years, even after the process of disillusionment had begun, are full of references to his continuing faith in democracy. In 1877 he wrote to his English friend, Charles Milnes Gaskell: "As I belong to the class of people who have great faith in this country and who believe that in another century it will be saying in its turn the last word of civilisation, I enjoy the expectation of the coming day." And in 1881 he could write to Wayne MacVeagh upon the occasion of Garfield's assassination: "Luckily we are a democracy and a sound one. Nothing can shake society with us, now that slavery is gone."

And the same essential faith in the American democratic ideal is implicit in Adams's novel, *Democracy,* despite its satiric rejection of the actualities of American government in 1879. There is no touch of irony in the speech which Adams puts into the mouth of his questing heroine, Mrs. Lightfoot Lee, when she takes it upon herself to chasten a young Italian Secretary of Legation who too easily accepts the idea that "there was no society except in the old world":

"Society in America? Indeed there is society in America and very good society too; but it has a code of its own, and newcomers seldom understand it. I will tell you what it is, Mr. Orsini, and you will never be in danger of making any mistake. 'Society' in America means all the honest, kindly mannered, pleasant-voiced women, and all the good, brave, unassuming men, between the Atlantic and the Pacific. Each of these has a free pass in every city and village, 'good for this generation only,' and it depends on each to make use of this pass or not as it may happen to suit his or her fancy. To this rule there are *no* exceptions, and those who say 'Abraham is our father' will surely furnish food for that humour which is the staple product of our country."

It rings, does it not, with the passionate naivety of an old-fashioned high-school oration, yet such sentiments about their country once served to aerate and brighten the minds of even the most sophisticated and critical of Americans—one finds them being uttered at a certain period by Henry James and with a passion of optimism no less naive than that of his friend Adams.

The awareness of this very attractive naivety of idealism is essential for the understanding of Adams's ultimate development in pessimism. It is endemic in *Democracy,* appearing in the use which is made of the simplicity and plainness of General Lee's house at Arlington, and in the elaborate discussion of Mount Vernon and General Washington as representing the republican virtues which, although receding into the past, are still part of the American dream.

In his introduction to the *Selected Letters,* Mr. Arvin refers to Adams's two anonymously published novels, *Democracy* and *Esther,* as "remarkable books, more remarkable than they have usually been recognized as being." And so they are. Of the two, *Democracy* is, I think, the more attractive. *Esther,* which stands in the same interrogative relation to religion that *Democracy* stands in to politics, is full of velleities of thought and feeling about its subject, and these, while possibly they make for an interesting darkness in the work, also make for uncertainty and irresolution. But *Democracy* is all clarity and brightness, and entirely satisfying so far as it goes. It does not, as a novel, go very far—does not pretend to go very far. It is brief and witty and schematic; everything in it is contrived and controlled by the author's intelligence and his gaiety. It can claim a degree of cousinage with Peacock's novels of intellectual humors; it shares the light speed of this form and it has more than a few Peacockian moments, such as that in which the bright young American heiress explains to a British visitor the trouble that Americans have with their sundials:

"Look at that one! they all behave like that. The wear and tear of our sun is too much for them; they don't last. My uncle, who has a place at Long Branch, had five sun-dials in ten years."
"How very odd! But really now, Miss Dare, I don't see how a sun-dial could wear out."
"Don't you? How strange! Don't you see, they get soaked with sunshine so that they can't hold shadow."

But although its humor is frequent and its wit pervasive, *Democracy* does not move among ideas with the Peacockian lack of commitment to anything but common sense. It is concerned to ask a question which was of the greatest importance to Adams himself, and to his countrymen: The nature of American political life being what it is, is it possible for a person of moral sensibility to participate in it?

The person upon whom the test is made is the attractive and intelligent young widow, Madeleine Lee—Adams is already, in middle life, making woman the touchstone and center of civilization. Bereaved of a husband and baby in a single year, Mrs. Lee has tried to fill her life with civilized interests, and, having found philosophy and philanthropy of no avail, has established herself in Washington intent on trying political activity as a last resort. "She wanted to see with her own eyes the action of primary forces; to touch with her own hand the massive machinery of society; to measure with her own mind the capacity of the motive power. She was bent upon getting to the heart of the great American mystery of democracy and government."

She wanted, in short, the experience of power, as did Adams himself. It was not merely her being a woman that brought it about that "the force of the engine was a little confused in her mind with that of the engineer, the power with the men who wielded it"; the confusion had existed in Adams's mind when he had decided that there was no possible place for him in American political life; the confusion is no confusion at all but an accurate statement of the fact.

Madeleine's experience of the men who wield the power, or try to wield it, is the substance of her sad education. Presidents of the United States, she learns, are likely to be foolish, vulgar, bedeviled men, who, with their impossible wives, lead the most hideous lives of public ceremony. Reformers maintain their equanimity only by a bland ignorance of the nature of what they are trying to change. Most senators are nonentities, and the one senator who is more than that, who does have the strength and craft to control the great machine, is, as poor Madeleine finds, venal—corrupt not merely through personal motives but by the acknowledged terms of his profession, by his devotion to party. And since it is this Senator Ratcliffe whom Madeleine is drawn to by reason of his power and even thinks of marrying, his acceptance and rationalization of his immorality is decisive with her. She surrenders Washington and withdraws from the political life, and the posed question is conclusively answered: No, it is not possible for a person of moral sensibility to take part in American politics.

Very likely the means by which the answer is made will seem too simple to us nowadays and not quite relevant to our situation— not that the moral probity of senators is now an article of our political faith, but that we do not take senatorial corruption for granted as it was taken for granted in the Seventies when Mark Twain instituted his famous comparison between the moral character of senators and that of hogs. But the question is still a valid one, and so, in some important part, is Adams's answer.

1952

The Novel Alive or Dead

EVERYBODY says that the novel is in a bad way and no doubt everybody is right. As long as two decades ago certain of the more recondite critics were telling us that the genre of the novel was quite played out, having reached its fullest possible development in Joyce and Proust. Now the speculation of criticism has become the harsh practicality of the publishing business—fiction, which once had the power to define all other forms of literature by creating that wondrous negative category of Non-Fiction, has lost its old prestige in the market. And within the last year or two the open secret of the publishing offices has been made available to the public, for in England and America it has become an almost institutional practice of literary journalism to propound the question whether the novel really is moribund, or to propose a symposium on its sad demise.

Consequently we are all in possession of the reasons why the novel is, or should be, or soon will be, dead. One reason commonly adduced is that the actuality of the world is so very intense and so very strange that the figments of the imagination cannot compete with it. It is now life and not art that requires the willing suspension of disbelief. Another reason is that two of the great subject-matters of the novel have been pre-empted by science—the novelist must compete as an unlicensed amateur with sociologists and psychologists, men who are intensively trained to tell us what is going on inside our social systems and our own breasts, with the result that the novelist has lost his once considerable status as an explorer and discoverer. Yet another reason advanced for the decline of the novel is that the mechanical techniques of drama are driving prose narrative from the field: the novel cannot compete with the lively immediacy of the cinema and television. And we are the more disposed to believe that this is so after we have followed Dr. Rudolf Flesch in his demonstration of how difficult, virtually impossible, it is to understand a sentence that ventures a subordinate clause, let alone a metaphor.

All this is cogent, and it is of course quite possible that the novel really is dead or dying. Particular forms of literature undoubtedly can die, or at least hibernate for long periods, and we shouldn't, out of sentimental attachment to the genre of the novel—after all, it did so much for us in our youth!—resist considering the possibility that it is not immortal and that its hour has struck. And yet, in the face of all evidence and argument, I am still not inclined to add my signature to the certificate of the novel's death. For, badly off as the novel may be, I cannot believe that its state is unique or exceptional: it is no worse off than a lot of other things in our culture. If, for example, we consider technical philosophy, we find that its condition is analogous to that of the novel—in academic circles it is generally understood that philosophy is in a seriously bad way, that its pulse is barely perceptible. What is true of philosophy is largely true of other intellectual disciplines, such as anthropology, sociology, and psychology. We see on all sides a notable refinement of techniques, and the number of gifted students and beginning practitioners is impressive. Yet it is impossible to be unaware of the intellectual somnolence that broods over these fields despite all the appearance of lively professional bustle. We are, it would seem, at a static moment of culture. Our will is puzzled and is much inclined to commit itself to a sort of neutralism. Naturally enough, this condition of doldrums makes itself especially apparent in the novel, which is the form of art evolved to deal with the complexities of the will. But doldrums do not last forever: the winds of doctrine will blow again.

At any rate, it seems to me that the situation is not quite hopeless that gives us C. P. Snow. Mr. Snow's novels, despite what some say, don't have upon them the mark of greatness, and it may well be that their author will never write a great novel. Those that he has written are very plain and modest, very businesslike in the way they go about engaging our emotions and intelligence. They make upon me the impression of having been written out of the express intention of proving that the novel is not dead. I find myself imagining the incident which launched Mr. Snow upon his career as a novelist. One evening a few years ago—so I fancy the scene—he was dining at his club and a member, a man he knew slightly and didn't much like, came up to him as he was leaving and remarked in a rather aggressive way that the novel was dead. Mr. Snow quietly replied that this wasn't how the case stood at all, that the member must have got his facts wrong. There followed a disagreement in which, although both men kept their tempers, feeling ran rather high. Four barristers, on their way to the card room, stopped to listen, as did an official of the BBC and the American guest he had in tow. They were joined by three civil servants, one of whom, as it later developed, was in contact with the Russian secret service. A club waiter, whose son was an under-secretary in the Ministry of Education, hovered on the fringes of the group. When the debate had gone on for some time, Mr. Snow's antagonist said with a sharpness that nobody quite liked, "Well, if you think it can be done, why don't you do it yourself?" For a moment there was shocked silence, for it was a strictly enforced rule of the club that no member might use an *ad hominem* argument. Then Mr. Snow said, "Very well, I will." His voice was strangely quiet. "Will you lay a wager on it?" said the other. "Will you bet? . . ." and he named a sum the loss of which would bring Mr. Snow to ruin and the Marshalsea. One of the barristers said, "Let it pass, Snow." And the BBC official said, "You'd be a fool to take him up." For it was not as if Mr. Snow were a literary man— he was a scientist, a physicist of solid reputation. But Mr. Snow did not heed these friendly warnings. "Done," he said quietly, and his face, as he put a match to his pipe, was every bit as imperturbable as Phileas Fogg's.

There remained, of course, the difficult business of deciding just what it was that Mr. Snow had undertaken to do. It was clear to everyone, even to Mr. Snow's opponent, that Mr. Snow had not committed himself to producing a work of genius. "That American fellow—what's his name?—Falconer?" said one of the civil servants. "Faulkner, sir," said the waiter. "Yes, that's what's I said. His sort of thing isn't the sort of thing that can be expected. Not that I *want* it, as I hope you understand. But it is, for good or bad, genius, and it isn't the sort of thing you can bet on, is it? Dostoievski either." "Or Joyce, or Proust, sir," said the waiter. "Exactly," said the civil servant. (He was not, incidentally, the one who was in touch with the Russians.)

After a good deal of discussion it was agreed that there was in the back of everyone's mind some simple, practical idea of the pleasure that might be had from reading a novel, and that this idea was not derived from the great works alone but from the mass of fiction, most of it eventually anonymous, which one read at an age when any story that had any verisimilitude, that seemed to bring us any information about the nature of life, was fascinating and delightful. "When," said the American guest, "there was no Henry James in our consciousness, no R. P. Blackmur, no F. R. Leavis; no notion of symbols; no idea of myth; no sense of the high isolate dignity of art; no college course in which the significance of the structure was demonstrated—just a mad rush of information about what might happen to us if we were lucky, about the possibility of the feeling we might some day experience, or the attitudes we might have a chance to strike." "Exactly—" said his host, "before we ever read novels in the high-toned American way—I *beg* you pardon." "Quite all right," said the American and went on to say that his own sense of the novel had been shaped by the Rover Boys, Horatio Alger, a few residual Hentys, *Little Women* (and all the inferior sequels), *The Light That Failed, Pendennis,* William J. Locke, *Trilby* and

Peter Ibbetson, The Passionate Friends (one of H. G. Wells's lesser efforts), and the infinite anonymity from the public library—it was these that had, as it were, made the way ready for Tolstoy, Dostoievski, and Proust. Not all the English were quite clear about all the items mentioned, but they accepted the list in principle, and Mr. Snow said that it was a sound principle.

That night in his rooms, rather frightened by what he had committed himself to, Mr. Snow took stock of his powers. No great gifts of language, of course. "I am a plain man," said Mr. Snow. No new theory of the novel. "Just begin at the beginning and go on to the end is the only way I know." No strange or violent or beautifully intense vision of life. No new notions of the moral life—on the contrary, a set of rather old-fashioned notions chiefly about loyalty and generosity. The best he could muster under the moral head was a belief that it was quite hard to live up to even these simple notions. "It is not much to make novels with," Mr. Snow thought.

But then it occurred to him that what he did have was a sense of social fact. Despite his being a scientist, he did have that. He really believed that society existed and that it was interesting—even crucial. He had a sense of the present in relation to a sense of the past, of the way things are and the way they used to be, and he found a significance in the difference between *now* and *then*. Then it seemed to him that he had a very strong interest in things that were nowadays being ruled out of the circle of legitimacy by some sort of tacit agreement. He was interested in Man in Committee, in man as he lives the petty politics of life, which he affects to despise and cannot, man looking for the small satisfactions of cash or prestige that his sons will despise before they begin to look for their own, the small successes or humiliations that are connected with one's part in some large event or institution which history will put in proper perspective or quite out of the picture—yet it is after all something that history will have to deal with, it has that much curious dignity.

And Mr. Snow tried to remember whether any novelist had gone into business with a capital anything like his. He found, of course,

Trollope—not the Trollope of the genteel cultists, the supposed cele-
brator of the peace of cathedral closes, the presumed ancestor of
Angela Thirkell, but the Trollope who saw rapid and violent
changes taking place in English society, the Trollope who is best
approached through *The Way We Live Now* rather than through
Barchester Towers, the great, unhurried observer of shifting morals
and manners.

"Well," said Mr. Snow, "one isn't, of course, Trollope. But a man
can do his best . . ."

The New Men is not, I think, quite so successful a novel as its
predecessor, *The Masters.* The earlier book has the advantage of a
more limited scene and action, with the result that it has a considerable power of implied meaning—the struggle for the Mastership of
a Cambridge college serves handsomely as a paradigm of the political
life. *The New Men,* in which certain characters of *The Masters* appear, including, of course, the narrator Lewis Eliot, is about the
work toward the atomic bomb, and the historical event is so momentous that it tends to minimize and disintegrate the personal
drama. Yet it does no more than tend this way—if it does not, like
the election in *The Masters,* generate partisan passions in us, it does
indeed lead us to commit to it our serious attention.

The phrase of the title is somewhat ambiguous in its reference.
Mr. Snow no doubt has in mind its Latin equivalent which the
Romans used in a pejorative way—the *novi homines* were the men
who challenged the old aristocracy, perhaps freedmen who had
gained commercial advantage. In Mr. Snow's title the phrase refers
chiefly to the scientists who have become a new element in public
life. But it has also a social sense, referring to men who, by their
talents, have risen from one or another of the lower classes. The
Eliots, Lewis the barrister and his brother Martin the physicist, are
from the "back streets of a lower-middle-class provincial town";
their mother was the daughter of a gamekeeper. Walter Luke, the
chief of the atomic project, had risen from the Plymouth dockyards.
Not the least interesting element of the novel is the observation of

how the differences of social origin are modified by the attitudes of the scientific group. Thus, all the physicists, no matter what their social origin, are at one in their alienation from the engineers, whom they regard as of a lower order. A scientist of whatever class is susceptible to Communist influence—Mr. Snow indicates admirably how the scientists' deficient sense of social fact, their disgust with the irrational contradictions of society, their strong but primitive sense of social good and responsibility, their feeling of being a class apart and discriminated against, serve to make them peculiarly susceptible to the moral imperatives around which the Communist ideology is built. Mounteney, the Nobel Prize winner, a man of the upper classes, is as simple in his response to the Communist appeal as the young beginner Sawbridge, whose background is the same as the Eliots' but who has not come to terms with his new class position. For Mounteney there is only one reason why atomic data should not be unofficially given to the Russians by any of the scientists who choose to—he is a man punctilious in honor and the group had taken an oath to impart information to no one. Sawbridge has no such punctilio, and it is he who actually does communicate information to the Russians, but the novel is at pains to represent him as a man having his own peculiar moral stamina, even his own sense of honor.

Here we must take note of one striking aspect of Mr. Snow's work, his lack of the impulse to blame. This is, we must suppose, not merely a personal but a national trait. Had *The Masters* been written by an American about an American university situation, we would surely have been given a struggle between virtue and corruption, or between liberalism and reaction, at the least between integrity and the lack of it. No American novelist could have easily tolerated an opposition which is chiefly between two temperaments with political and cultural values merely implicit in it. The American impulse to blame is very strong. Had *The New Men* been written by an American about an American situation, either the Communist scientists, or the Government, or the security agency would have been shown to be malign and contemptible. As Mr. Snow handles his situation he goes so far in his surrender of the impulse, or the desire, or the right to blame that he leads me to wonder whether he doesn't go too far in general pardon—when he speaks of the "progressive" scientists having made a choice between Hitler and Communism, choosing Communism because, if it did ill, it did ill "that good might come" and goes on to say that these men "could not change all the shadows of these thoughts in an afternoon," I can't help thinking of the failure of intelligence that was involved with the good will, of the laziness of scientific minds that interpreted so badly the inadequately-gathered evidence, of the arrogance of scientific minds that were sure that politics and human good are so easily comprehended. Yet when I have exercised my disagreeable American prerogative of blame, I recognize how essential to Mr. Snow's enterprise is his tendency to forgiveness, how liberating it is, how it is a condition of the reality of his characters.

A word more about the title of Mr. Snow's novel: it is an accurate title—his new men really are new, they are novel, and that is why they make a novel. It may be that they are not perceived in the greatest possible profundity, but they are seen accurately in the novelty of their personal quality, in the novelty of their relation to themselves, and to each other, to intellect, to society, to the state. It is the news, the *nouvelle,* about them that guarantees the great interest of Mr. Snow's novel.

1955

Criticism and Aesthetics

OVER the last few decades the branch of philosophy which goes under the uncertain name of aesthetics has lost much of its once-considerable hold upon our interest. I do not mean, of course, that the questions of aesthetics do not continue to be asked and the answers valiantly attempted—any bibliography of the subject will show the contrary to be true. But the professional concern with these questions does not nowadays, as once it did, overflow its academic banks to fertilize the broad plain of the general culture.

One might easily suppose that the contrary would be true. With the enormous elaboration of modern artistic theory and practice, with our ever-growing awareness of foreign cultures radically different from our own in their assumptions about art, it might well have been expected that the general interest in a unifying aesthetic theory would have become greater rather than less. And perhaps there are signs that this is coming to be the case. Yet I think it is still true to say that aesthetics is looked at askance by people who are neither indifferent to art nor hostile to theoretical discussion.

Aesthetics is, at least in one established definition of its meaning, the theory of the Beautiful. And when we think of the present situation of aesthetics, we must take into account the disrepute into which the Beautiful has fallen. We are not likely to speak of beauty when we praise the art we most admire. We perceive, indeed, that a great many of the most notable art-works of our time consciously repel the use of the word—one of the inceptive impulses of modern art was a fierce impatience with beauty as it was understood by an earlier age and as it still lingers in our minds to make us dubious and uneasy in our references to it. We feel that the concept of beauty implies a harmony too easily achieved, and even a degree of softness and luxuriousness which we resent. Our notion of beauty is haunted by the shade of Winckelmann, with its preference for the fluid, softly curved line, its dislike of angularities and tensions, its contempt for all art that did not conform to the canons of a Greek period already, as we judge it, decadent. We feel, too, that the beauty of the nineteenth-century aestheticians is too much controlled by the example of Aristotle's discussion of tragedy; we resist its tendency to suggest that the elements of harshness and pain in a work of art are present only that they may be overcome in reconciliation and peace, and that the perfect aesthetic effect is repose. It is not hard to see why Ogden and Richards won a very quick assent when, some thirty years ago, they said that beauty was a concept rather worse than useless, that it stood in the way of our right response to art, and that it had better yield to the criterion of *interest*.

But the discussion of art is a human activity quite as natural as the creation of art, and our loss of confidence and interest in aesthetics did not bring the discussion of art to an end. The preferred form of discourse about art became that of criticism. The modern movement of criticism began with a sense of happy escape from the large generalizations of aesthetics, with the enthusiasm of getting down—at last!—to business, to brass tacks, to—precisely—cases. Not Art but the particular work of art became the preoccupation of our discourse. Criticism could not, of course, proceed without general aesthetic ideas, but these were now chiefly of an implicit sort, and they made but little reference to beauty.

This tendency was no doubt necessary and good, yet it produced one result that may be deplored. The criterion of *interest* is one that is peculiarly applicable to literature; and literary criticism came to be pre-eminent above the criticism of any of the other arts. It dominated the whole of our discourse about art. Our artistic culture has become chiefly, almost exclusively, a literary culture. It is a fact of capital importance, which scarcely anyone remarks on, let alone finds reason to be troubled by, that our critical journals give no room to the criticism of music and the plastic arts, that there is little or no commerce between literary people on the one hand and painters and musicians on the other. So that, while no doubt there is acceptance of the non-literary arts and they may even be said in some sense to "flourish," there is no real response to them on the part of people to whom the idea of art, and the actuality of literary art, mean a good deal. I hesitate to make the affirmation in the face of the eminent literary critics who have recently been telling us how useless a thing criticism is and how it stands in the way of our appreciation of the work of art itself, but the fact is that an actual response to art (in our culture at least) depends on discourse—not upon any one kind of discourse, but upon discourse of *some* kind. The silent acceptance of, say, contemporary painting by most educated people is in part the result of habituation, but it is also the result of intimidated indifference. If they were really responding to the actuality of the pictures, they would be very nearly as quarrelsome about them as the painters themselves.

This relative indifference to other arts than literature is, as I say, in some part the result of the loss of authority which has been suffered by general aesthetic theory. When we dismiss the no doubt vague concepts of general aesthetic theory, when we get rid of the idea of beauty and rely on the idea of *interest,* we make it very difficult for important elements of the experience of art to find expression, and we open the way for literary criticism to take possession of the whole field of our concern with art. The abstractness and difficulty of the concepts of aesthetics suggest, however inadequately, something of the mystery of art. And literary criticism, by and large, does not have much truck with mystery—it has no need to. In its handling of the criterion of *interest* it is very much at ease, and it is always driving toward the cognate criterion of *cogency*. Not, it may be granted, by reason of the essence of literature but certainly by reason of prevailing accident, the judgment of literature is overtly and explicitly a moral and intellectual judgment. The cogency, the appositeness, the logicality, the *truth* of ideas must always be passed upon by literary criticism. Aestheticians, and some literary critics, are in a sweat to set limits upon this mode of judgment. They are committed to the idea that the aesthetic experience is characterized by its remoteness from considerations of practicality, and they tell us that literature is an art like any other, and that the right experience of it shares this general characteristic of the aesthetic experience, that considerations of practicality—morality and truth—are essentially irrelevant. Alas! literature seems always to be telling us the opposite. As against its own purely aesthetic elements, it is always mustering the reminders of the practical—of the mundane, the dirty, the ugly, the painful, the moral—and it does so very consciously: Jane Austen's objection to *Pride and Prejudice,* that it was too perfect, too unified and harmonious in its style, that its perfection needed to be ravished by the presence of something actual and dull and doctrinal, ought to be framed over the desk of every aesthetician and critic. Literature doesn't easily submit to the category of aesthetic contemplative dis-interestedness—so much of it insists *"De* TE *fabula*—this means *you,"* and often goes on to say, "And you'd better *do* something about it quick." Time and tradition diminish our awareness of literature's nasty unaesthetic tendency to insist upon some degree of immediate practicality, and the aestheticians take all possible advantage of this effect of time and tradition. But if human experience—human danger and pain—is made the material of an artistic creation, the judgment that is directed upon the creation will involve important considerations of practicality and thus of cogency, relevance, apposite-ness, logicality, and truth. Unless we get the clear signal from the literary work itself that we are not to ask the question, we inevitably do ask, "Is this true, is this to be believed, is this to shape our future judgments of experience?" And even when the literary work does give us the clear signal that we are not to apply this standard, we are sure to ask some such question as, "What is being implied about logic and truth by this willful departure from logic and truth?"

No one who takes literature seriously will wish to minimize the importance and the rightness of this mode of judgment, not unless he is tempted by the charms of general aesthetic theory to try to bring the experience of literature into a theoretical conformity with the experience of the other arts. And yet the mode of judgment which is entirely appropriate to literature, if it comes to seem to us the sole mode of artistic judgment, or the predominant or controlling mode, will have the effect of severely limiting our experience of the other arts.

This was borne in upon me by a reading of Louis Arnaud Reid's admirable book, *A Study of Aesthetics,* and by one passage in particular. I shall characterize the whole work more fully in a moment, but what first struck me as remarkable about it was the effect it produced of liberation and enlargement, of the widening of the aesthetic response beyond the limits to which we have become habituated. In the passage to which I refer, Dr. Reid is speaking, by way of example, of a spoon, "a large shallow-bowled spoon with a silver handle," which has delighted him.

The lines are smooth, easy, liquid, flowing; the handle is deliciously curved, like the tail of a leopard. And strangely, without contradiction, the leopard's tail is finished with little raised nodules like small grapes. It is a queer mixture of a leaf and a leopard. The texture is grey and dull like river mist, and it is lit with soft lights shining out of it like the moon out of a misty sky. The sheen is white-grey satin: the bowl is delicately shaped with overturning fastidiously pointed fronds; it is restrained and shallow, yet large enough to be generous. The lines are fine and sharp, with clear edges. Thus described, such a concatenation of qualities may sound absurd and incongruous. But if you hold the spoon in your hand, you feel it as a kind of poem, which in a strange way unites all these, and many other, values into a single whole. You feel as you see it that you are living in a gracious world, full of loveliness and delight.

Now this, of course, is not an example of aesthetic theory. It is criticism, and criticism of a kind that we have been taught to be suspicious of—it is "impressionistic" or "appreciative" criticism. What is more, it is "literary," perhaps in several ways but especially because it is so quick to discover the "moral" of the spoon—the spoon suggests a "gracious" world. The method of description which is used is one that might easily be used for the description of a poem, and indeed it sometimes is so used; yet the passage implies something more and something different from what literary criticism is likely to imply about our experience of art—it imputes to the beholder an experience more immediate, more physical and less intellectual, or, perhaps better, more physical-intellectual, and to the object itself more power, and to the conjunction of the object and the beholder more mystery. And this, I think, is likely to be the effect that discourse upon art makes when it is liberated, by the impulse to formulate a general aesthetic theory, from the predominant literary category of cogency.

Dr. Reid is an English philosopher, a member of the University of London. *A Study of Aesthetics,* which grew out of a series of lectures given by Dr. Reid at the University of California, is not a new work, having first been published in 1931. But the fact that it does not take account of the developments of aesthetic theory in the intervening time does not seem to me to be a disadvantage to the general reader seeking an introduction to the subject; it may even be thought of as an advantage. Much the same thing can be said of the fact that, at the time at which he wrote, Dr. Reid seems to have been reached by relatively little of the modern movement in any of the arts. His examples of the plastic arts are from the older masters; in music Debussy is his latest reference; and in poetry he seems to take cognizance of very little after the Georgians. But this does not limit the pertinence of his generalizations. On the contrary, indeed, for it makes an interesting and useful intellectual exercise to perceive how Dr. Reid's formulations, based on traditional works, are valid and illuminating when applied to contemporary art.

In the manner of its presentation, the book is exemplary. Its prose is direct, clear, lively, and even witty; and it is notably good-natured, which is always a virtue in philosophical prose. Yet it does not attempt the rather ghastly "common touch" which some philosophers, particularly the English, have recently been cultivating. ("Myfanwy has bought a new plaid dress and Robin tells Myfanwy that he doesn't like it. We can understand Robin's remark to mean one of three—and perhaps four—things. Either, etc.") Wherever it is possible to be simple, Dr. Reid is simple; and where the exigencies of the subject make it impossible for him not to be difficult—"dull," as he puts it—Dr. Reid says so.

To follow Dr. Reid's exposition in detail is scarcely possible in an essay of this kind—I can at most suggest the intellectual temper and something of the scope of the volume. As to its intellectual temper, this can best be implied by reference to a remark of Roger Fry's which Dr. Reid quotes. "Biologically speaking," Fry said, "art is a blasphemy. We were given our eyes to see things with, not to look at them." Fry, of course, is referring to the distinction between the "practical" and the "disinterested" which aesthetic theory always takes account of; it is an idea as necessary to aesthetics, and just as dangerous, as his heel was to Achilles. Dr. Reid himself accepts the distinction, but he will have nothing to do with Fry's formulation of it—so far from understanding the aesthetic experience to be biological blasphemy, he understands it to be rooted in biology. The aesthetic experience, according to one definition of it that Dr. Reid offers, involves the perception of an object in such a way "that it appears in its very qualities and form to express or embody valuable meaning." But this mode of perception is indigenous to the mind, to "body-and-mind," as Dr. Reid says we must think of it, which takes all sense-data as being in some degree expressive. We perceive colors, shapes, and tones as having, in some sort, meaning and value. This experience Dr. Reid calls "direct aesthetic experience"; it is not of the same order as the experience of a work of art, but it defines the nature of the mind that does have the experience of the work of art, that requires and enjoys such experience—it defines the mind as value-perceiving and value-bestowing. The stipulation of value-perceiving is important, for Dr. Reid resists the temptations of radical subjectivity. He will not admit that it is merely by the associations which cultural habit enforces upon us that we find colors, shapes, and tones to be expressive. Although value and meaning are given by the mind, the mind cannot give value and meaning indiscriminately—certain *sensa,* and not others, can support certain values and meanings, and not others.

His position, that is to say, has much in common with that of Wordsworth, who insisted that meanings and values were to be found in the conjunction of a mind that could discover values with an object that could generate them—a view in marked opposition to that of the more radically subjective Coleridge. And it is therefore appropriate that, in his final chapter, Dr. Reid should face boldly what he calls "The Enigma of Natural Beauty," the troublesome questions of whether or not the experience of natural beauty is properly to be regarded as a true aesthetic experience, and of in how far the large meanings that are likely to be derived from this experience are valid. Such an inquiry is implicit in Dr. Reid's understanding of the enterprise of aesthetics—early in his book Dr. Reid says of aesthetic theory that, while it must indeed take account of the sense-pleasure of the aesthetic experience, it "must also account for those aesthetic experiences which seem to shake the very foundation of our being. The temple is a pile of stones, the symphony a conglomeration of sounds, the dance a set of movements. But these possess meanings for aesthetic contemplation which it is beyond words to describe. It is beyond words to describe them, not merely because they may appear profound as life itself, but because they are in their essence untranslatable, being just the embodied meanings of stones, sounds, movements. To understand the nature of this embodiment in its untranslatableness is to understand the essence of aesthetic." Here, of course, is the recognition of the mystery of the experience of art which literary criticism does indeed formally recognize but which, by reason of its own task, it is likely to obscure.

From even the little I have said of Dr. Reid's first principles, it might be expected that he will take, as indeed he does, a large, open, and generous view of the aesthetic experience. Like any aesthetician, he is concerned to maintain the singularity of the aesthetic experience, to differentiate it both from the practical and from the other experiences of pleasure which might encroach upon it. But although he affirms the uniqueness of the aesthetic experience, he is not worried about its "purity." Nothing could be more sensible and liberating than the license which Dr. Reid grants himself and us to allow personal and historical associations, irrational attachments and affections, to take their place as legitimate elements of the aesthetic experience. (See, on page 105 of his book, his happy remarks on another piece of silverware, a fat Victorian teapot.) His differentiation of the aesthetic from the practical does not lead him to overlook the passional nature of aesthetic experience, its "needs" and "demands," its being a "life of appetite and satisfaction."

On the relation of technique to imagination he is remarkably lucid, and he is equally good and clear on the vexed question of imitation. I could wish that, since he felt it necessary to raise the question of the place of the unconscious in the process of creation and in the aesthetic experience, he had done so with less conventional resistance to the idea, and also that less conventionality marked his treatment of the subject of unity in art, for this canon of judgment gives a larger handle to stupidity than almost any other and ought to be dealt with radically and even explosively. But long before it was decent to question the idea that fulfillment of function guarantees the aesthetic value of an object, Dr. Reid had the courage to do so and with admirable modulation. And no one could open with more tact than he has done the dreadful and delightful questions of the relation of art to truth and reality and to moral values.

In the course of his definition and defense of the enterprise of the aesthetic philosopher which constitutes his introductory chapter Dr. Reid says:

Having emphasized, then, that the business of the aesthetic philosopher is intellectual analysis and construction, and that, in order to analyse and construct to any purpose, he must also have first-hand acquaintance with beautiful things, we may now turn to meet the objections . . . to the philosopher's making any attempt at all to analyse beautiful things.

The most direct—and perhaps the final—answer that can be given to the question, Why analyse? is that we have a fundamental impulse to do it, that we usually do it badly, and that if done at all it ought to be done well. Everyone has notions about what art or beauty is, even although these notions never become expressed in words. We do not merely feel, we think also. And it is unanalysed notions and preconceptions which, entering into our feelings about beautiful things, more often than not mislead us and induce false attitudes towards them. If we are to have preconceptions at all—and we can never avoid having them—then it is surely better, if opportunity offers itself, that we should take a little trouble in trying to acquire true preconceptions for future occasions. These true preconceptions are worth acquiring for their own sake, for the sake of their truth, but it is almost certain that in the end they also help us to appreciate more truly.

The case could not be put better. I would add only this particularity, that at this time our response to art stands in peculiar need of the quickening and liberating influence of aesthetic theory. There is no book more likely to establish for the general reader the interest and importance of that theory or better fitted to give him its elements than Dr. Reid's humane and elegant *Study*.

1954

On Not Talking

[An address at a dinner meeting of the National
Institute of Arts and Letters.]

WHEN I was asked by our secretariat to provide a title for
my talk this evening, I deliberately chose a dark phrase,
one that would disclose nothing of my actual intention.
For the sordid fact is that I had it in mind, and have it still in mind,
to talk about a very old, worn-out subject, one that has long since
fatigued your interest. I mean to speak of the alienation of the
American artist and intellectual.

But perhaps it will be an extenuation of this dullness of mine if I
say that I am not going to talk about the alienation of the American
artist and intellectual from the general culture of his nation, from
the great mass of his fellow-citizens who are not themselves artists
or intellectuals. I mean to talk about his alienation from his own
class, by which I mean a very simple thing, our habit of not talking
to each other.

In the image of the artist that has developed since, say, the
Romantic period, there are two opposing elements. One of these
represents the creative man as being, in the very nature of his calling,
an alienated man, or at least an isolated man. This characterization
reflects, of course, the inescapable conditions of his kind of work.
He works alone: in very few of the artistic professions is collabora-
tion or company possible in the act of creation. Then he must always
aim at originality, even uniqueness; what he makes must be different
from what is made by any other man. That is one reason why he

conceives of his life history as being a long experience of misunderstanding and rejection. And that is why, too, he conceives his real reward as consisting in a new and more gratifying kind of isolation: for fame is indeed a kind of isolation, an acknowledgment of the artist's successful effort to be unique. The scientist also loves fame, but illicitly; it is not in accord with his professional legend that he should do so, and he is ashamed if his guilty passion is discovered. But the poet has always frankly avowed his love of fame because it is, really, an extension of his necessary desire to be unique; because, too, his success is to be measured by the suffrage of the world. And the poet's desire for fame is shared by the practitioners of all the creative arts.

And so we have the representation of the creative man as living at a distance from his kind—in nineteenth-century poetry he is likely to be represented as living on a mountain top, Zarathustra-fashion. Thus is represented his removal from the mundane concerns of men, and also, no doubt, his nearness to the divine creativity; some day he will come down from that mountain bearing in his hands the heavy tablets of the Law. But of course it might be a lonely cottage in a vale that he inhabits; or he may be thought of as living in essential solitude in his study or studio in the very midst of the bustle of some great city, or at night, wakeful while all the world sleeps. In any case he fulfills his entelechy, that law of his being which requires him to live alone.

The other aspect of the image of the artist and intellectual represents him as having a particular love of the idea of community. He has a special talent for community because he is thought not to be moved by the considerations of material competitiveness which are the mainspring of the actions of ordinary men. It is part of his ideal character to be delighted by humanity in its ideal character; he cannot live with the Philistines, but he aspires to live in community with the Children of Light. And so we see, in the nineteenth century, that at some point or other in the lives of many artists and intellectuals there is likely to be a period when the idea of community, of a sharing of all things, is of the highest importance in their conception of themselves. The Pantisocracy did not materialize, but the group around Wordsworth and Coleridge thought of itself as a special community of like mind and heart. Byron and Shelley at Pisa have the intention of constituting their own protected society. Flaubert lived at Croisset in solitude—in, if you will, alienation—but the dinners with the famous company of his friends at Magny's restaurant were the very breath of life to him. The generalization of this urge to community is Bohemia—that mythical polity which is ruled by nothing but a sentiment, the sentiment of generosity, of love and fellow feeling. And certainly it is true that the history of nineteenth-century art and intellect may be told as the history of friendships.

It was as part of this very intense feeling for personal community that the artists and writers of the age conceived of the community of the arts. We in our day also hold a very high opinion of the community of the arts, but in a different way—in the way of panel-discussions, arranged perhaps by some great Foundation, which, overcome by the idea that unity is a good thing, undertakes to bring together representatives of the various arts who will, there is no doubt of it, make the wonderful discovery that all the arts have some of the same presuppositions, that all the arts have at heart the good and the pleasure of mankind, and that all the arts should be encouraged and supported by all good men. This is not how the community of the arts was understood in the nineteenth century. The idea then was that the community was based in the natural fellowship of mind, of the creative imagination; it was a personal community.

If you look at the journal of Delacroix or merely at Walter Pach's introduction to his translation of it—the book, published in 1937 by the firm of Covici, Friede, is one of the handsomest pieces of American bookmaking—you will very quickly see what I mean. Delacroix was one of the very greatest geniuses of modern times. His influence on painting has been enormous. As Mr. Pach says in his introduction, "The discoveries of the Impressionists as to the relation of light and color are based on study of Delacroix; Renoir and Cézanne are deeply influenced by him; Van Gogh makes variants of his pictures; Seurat ponders deeply over his aesthetics; Matisse and Derain are devoted upholders of his authority." One of the striking things about Delacroix is the passion of catholicity which marks his effort to develop and perfect his own art. He has none of the exclusivism about traditions of art which we today are likely to consider a virtue, a kind of chastity. He levies with consummate freedom upon the schools of the past and of the present. It is not that he is what we call eclectic in the common pejorative sense of that word. It is rather that his penetrating mind sees beyond the conventional categories to the essentials of genius. Then it is worth observing that he does not, at the behest of intuition, or of the passion of creativity, or of the ideal of the painter's *métier,* hold himself aloof from conscious intellect. This man in frail health, whose paintings make a body of work of vast size, also lays claim to a great canon of aesthetic theory, some of which is embodied in several volumes of essays, most in notes in the very extensive journal; these notes on theory were written toward that huge Dictionary of the Fine Arts which Delacroix contemplated but never achieved.

What next engages our notice is the range of his interest beyond painting, although to be sure every interest came back to painting. Architecture, of course; music, which he discussed with his friend Chopin—Beethoven was one of his devotions, as was Mozart, whom he brought together in a striking comparison with Virgil. And then, perhaps most especially, literature. No one will call Delacroix a literary painter despite his persistently literary subject matter, but literature is deeply involved with all his ideas about style and he loved to talk about it—with Balzac, with Gautier, with George Sand. And literature responded to him in a way that we know. Goethe said of Delacroix's illustrations for *Faust* that they had re-created his meaning. Baudelaire gave him homage, and came to the defense of his draughtsmanship, saying what must have seemed strange at the time, that only two men in Paris could draw as well as Delacroix— Ingres and Daumier. The admiration given to him by Taine, that now too much neglected man, was of the highest.

I speak of Delacroix not in order to praise his genius, although that is pleasant to do, but to use him as an example, extreme but not unique, of the life of the community of the arts. This community grows less and less with the years, especially in this country. If I speak only of the art of literature, I am dismayed, as I look back to the period I have been talking about, and make the comparison between then and now, by the tenuity of the relationship that exists between literature and painting, or between literature and architecture, or between literature and music. I speak of the tenuity of the relationship, but it may be questioned if any relationship exists at all.

How significant a fact it is that our advanced magazines, which have conceived it to be their function to deal with our cultural life in general, deal less and less, and scarcely ever, with any other art than literature. These magazines have a very hard life, as I know through association with them, and we cannot fairly blame them; it is not as if they were indifferent. The editors, if questioned about their silence on painting and music, will reply, no doubt with truth and justice, that they cannot find the experts who write well enough or are willing to write for a lay public; and, they might add, for a public that is not very responsive to discourse on the non-literary arts. But of course, it is not only the experts who should be looked to—it is the novelists, poets, and literary critics who, overleaping the frontier barriers of *expertise,* should rush in where experts fear to tread. Leaving aside the question of his genius, what training did Baudelaire have that made him the best critic of painting of his day, that allowed him to defend Delacroix's draughtsmanship by comparison with Ingres and Daumier when (as Mr. Pach reminds us) all the experts could think this a foolish or a paradoxical statement, Ingres being the chief of the school from which Delacroix revolted, Daumier being nothing but a newspaper cartoonist?

I am not, I should make plain, putting blame exclusively on my own profession of literature. It may be that literature has a special degree of responsibility for the community of the arts, but literature is not solely responsible. It is my sense of the matter that blame attaches to all the artistic and intellectual professions. We are not members each of the other. We prefer not to talk to each other.

Now, between one art and another there must always be a gulf fixed, great or small. Despite what I have said about the large catholicity of Delacroix's mind, and the large catholicity of the artistic culture in which he lived, it is not true that the artist can be what is meant in theories of higher education when they refer to the Whole Man. An artist is not a Whole Man, and should not be—the nature of his commitment implies a specialness, a concentration, an exclusion of certain ways of being. This may be freely granted—I should even want to insist on it. It has, however, nothing to do with the sense of the community of the arts, which is a good in itself, as well as a favorable condition for the development of every art.

If we ask ourselves why it is that the community of the arts has so diminished with us, certain answers come very readily to mind. Perhaps they are not the less true because they are so pat.

The first explanation that occurs to us is the intense specialization of the arts and the intellectual disciplines which has taken place, and the difficulty of apprehension this entails. But I am not sure that this explanation isn't merely another way of describing the situation, rather than a discovery of what causes it.

Then there is the matter of time, and this is certainly of great importance. Who can possibly have time for the awareness of any but his own kind of work? It is one of the most obvious facts of nature that time has changed since the nineteenth century, and that we haven't enough of it to devote to community. What brought about this change is hard to know. Anxiety, some will say, and they may be right. Anxiety may have resulted in some diminution in the readiness of our wits; and time, for a creative mind, is measured by the motor power of his creative apparatus: the slower it is, the faster time goes. If you have the free creativity of Delacroix you can spend all Sunday, March 4th, 1849, reading Thackeray's *Vanity Fair;* on Monday the 5th you spend time with Meissonier in his studio; on Tuesday the 6th you are at a concert, ravished by the choruses from

Mozart's *Idomeneo;* on Thursday the 8th you visit Chopin, who is dying; on Saturday the 10th you call on an acquaintance to look at his Dürers and some Leonardo sketches; on Sunday you go to hear Beethoven's *Pastoral Symphony;* on Monday the 12th to see Rachel perform *Athalie.* Two days later to dinner at the home of Véron; Rachel is of the company; you chat with General Rullière, the minister of war, about *Athalie,* you talk about music with Armand Bertin and then about Racine and Shakespeare. And you have time to record these events in your diary—and more than these, for Mr. Pach has selected among the entries—and to set down your expansive and vivacious reflections upon them. If you are, say, Dickens, with his free creativity, you can not only afford to die in your prime, but you can also afford to dine out, and edit magazines and newspapers, and arrange testimonial dinners and receive them, and put on plays and act in them, and walk half the night with a friend, and carry on a huge correspondence by hand, and engage in charitable enterprises, and know everybody, artists, lawyers, physicians, engineers, and learn something from them all. Maybe the change in time came about as a result of our rapidity of mechanical communications and of labor-saving devices. Whatever the reason, I think it is true that time has changed and that this diminution of the dimension of time is a possible cause of a diminution of community in the arts.

Yet I am inclined to find a more definitive reason elsewhere—in certain assumptions of our culture about personality, and in our manners.

For having used that word *manners* in one or two of my essays I have been scolded more than once. One writer went so far as to throw the book at me, the volume being a Miss Vanderbilt's elaborate work on etiquette. The idea was that this is what I really meant by manners, and very snobby and genteel of me it was. But my teacher in this matter isn't Miss Vanderbilt but Alexis de Tocqueville. In his great book on American democracy Tocqueville makes manners integral with culture and here is the way he begins a chapter called "Some Reflections on American Manners": "Nothing seems at first sight less important than the outward form of human actions. Yet there is nothing by which men set more store; they grow used to everything except to living in a society which has not their own manners." And he goes on to say that although manners are "sometimes the result of an arbitrary convention between certain men," they are "generally the product of the very basis of character."

It is of manners as the product of the very basis of character that I would speak.

The manners that prevail in the life of intellect and art are very important because they have to deal with a very strenuous situation. W. B. Yeats says somewhere—in one of his autobiographies, I believe —that the religious life is to be distinguished from the intellectual and artistic life in this way: that the religious life says we are all alike, no one better than another, but the life of intellect and art says "Thou fool." Now of course there is no system of manners that might possibly be invented that can accommodate this utterance of the artistic and intellectual life. Here Delacroix has something to say to the point; he was a man of strong opinions and strong character, but he set great store by amenity. "That so-called frankness," he says, "which permits people to utter cutting or wounding opinions is the thing for which I have the greatest possible antipathy. Relationships among men are no longer possible if frankness like that is a sufficient answer to everything." In the artistic and intellectual professions especially there may be differences of theory and practice so great and so deeply and intricately bound up with our views of our very selves and of other selves that the only possible, the only human, way of dealing with them, in actual social intercourse, is to ignore them entirely, to pray that both parties will discover their common interest in African violets.

Yet when one has paid full tribute to amenity, one cannot but be aware of the consequences of the American horror of intellectual disagreement. Those of us who live in universities will, I am sure, recognize the following formula, and no doubt others will recognize it too. Professor Mumbleton, a fine scholar, *loquitur:* "We are all very grateful for what Professor Bumbleford has given us in his spendid talk. He has formulated for us what has been going on in the minds of several of us for some time. There are a few comments that I should like to make on what Professor Bumbleford has said but I should like to say first that I am in essential agreement with the direction of Professor Bumbleford's thinking, and if I seem to disagree with him, it is only by way of suggesting that there are certain changes of emphasis that might fruitfully be made. I want to stress that it is only a different emphasis that I shall emphasize in these comments—for that's all they are, just comments—and that I'm not making a criticism of the essential direction of his thinking."

The assumption of the speaker is that Professor Bumbleford will be destroyed, wiped out, annihilated, if the direction of his thinking is disagreed with—notice, by the way, that Mumbleton ascribes to Bumbleford not *ideas,* but *thinking:* that is to say, a process of thought rather than the product of thought; Mumbleton means to make Bumbleford's situation the more comfortable, for if thought is in process, its "direction" can be reversed, the thinker can yet save himself from being—God help him!—*wrong.* All this isn't very flattering to the man who is being disagreed with—it isn't very flattering to assume that your opponent is in danger of being snuffed out by your disagreement. But this, of course, is just what Mumbleton feels about himself—*he,* he knows, *would* cease to exist if he were disagreed with; the same must be true of Bumbleford. His manner is not that of courtesy, which so fierce an intellectual antagonist as Nietzsche made one of the intellectual virtues; it is a mere device of self-protection.

Not many of us can aspire to the charm of William James which made it possible for him to express radical disagreement—I will not say without some degree of violence done to the other person's feelings, but without any intimation of disrespect: with, on the contrary, the strong intimation that the disagreement is based on the greatest respect. But little as we may have James's gift, as we read James's letters in which he expresses disagreement, those, for example, in which he condemns, quite mistakenly, his brother's practice of the art of the novel, or undertakes to refute the system of a philosophical colleague, we cannot but feel that this is the right tone of the intellectual life. There is in James's superb manners in disagreement (as in agreement) a certain innocence, now lost from American life, a certain respect for his fellow-man that transcends any question of mere status or prestige in the social or intellectual community.

Another way of speaking of James's innocence is to say that he was not afraid of turning out to be wrong, or a fool; and if he did turn out to be a fool, he was going to enjoy a fool's prerogative, which is, of course, to rush in where angels fear to tread. That is why, no doubt, he cultivated the manner of a divine amateur: he wanted to dispel the air of secrecy that attends all established professions. He walked out of painting and into psychology by way of medicine, and from psychology into philosophy, all with the fine air of there being nothing *arcane* in any subject, although there may be much that is difficult.

The particular gift of intellectual grace with which William James was endowed is, as I say, not granted to most of us. Yet what that grace grows from, innocence, a readily given personal respect, a carelessness about being wrong, or stupid—this is something for us to be aware of as a condition of mind that may be cultivated. If we ask what it is that at the present time is the most discouraging element of American cultural life, I think we might conclude that it is not indifference, or a vulgar materialism, or a settled hostility to art and intellect, none of the things of which the class of artists and intellectuals usually accuses the great public, but rather a lack of innocence and ready human respect, a fear of being wrong, an aspiration to *expertise*. And I think that it may be worth remarking to an audience such as this, to the membership of our Institute, that what might be said of our public might also be said of us as representatives of our class, we with our carefully sustained separateness of one art from the other, we with our lack of curiosity about each other's art—I am sure you will understand that what I say is not intended as a criticism; I am in entire agreement with every other point of view; I am just kicking the idea around; merely trying it on for size; I am only trying to emphasize (or shall I say stress?) what might possibly need emphasis (or stress). But then again, of course, it might not. . . .

1955

"That Smile of Parmenides Made Me Think"

ONE doesn't have to read very far in Santayana's letters to become aware that it might be very hard to like this man— that, indeed, it might be remarkably easy to dislike him. And there is no point in struggling against the adverse feeling. The right thing to do is to recognize it, admit it into consciousness, and establish it beside that other awareness, which should come as early and which should be the stronger of the two—that Santayana was one of the most remarkable men of our time and that his letters are of classic importance.

To say that they are among the best of modern letters is not to say much, if anything. I can think of no modern collections of letters—D. H. Lawrence's and Shaw's excepted—that aren't deeply depressing in their emptiness and lack of energy, in their frightening inability to suggest living spirit. To find an adequate point of comparison for Santayana's letters one has to go back to the nineteenth century. Santayana isn't, of course, equal to Keats as a letter writer, but that one can even think to say that he isn't is considerable compliment. I am led to make the comparison not because the letters of Santayana and of Keats are similar in kind but because they are similar in effect. No recent book has taken possession of my mind as this one has, commanding not assent (or not often) but concurrence—I mean a literal "running along with," the desire to follow where the writer leads. One of the effects of Keats's letters is to suggest that the writer holds in his mind at every moment a clear image of the actual quotidian world and also an image of the universe and of a mode of existence beyond actuality yet intimately related to actuality and, in a sense, controlling it. I don't pretend to understand Santayana's doctrine of essences, not having read the works in which he expounds it; nor, indeed, do I wholly understand Keats's doctrine of essences, although I do perceive that it was central to his thought. I suspect that the two doctrines have much in common and I recommend the exploration of this possibility to a competent philosopher. But quite apart from any connection that may be found between Santayana's thought and Keats's—it was certainly not an influence: Santayana read Keats in the old nineteenth-century way, and was skeptical of the idea that Keats *thought* at all—what one finds in the two men as letter writers is the force and seduction of their manner of thought, their impulse to think about human life in relation to a comprehensive vision of the nature of the universe.

It is this that accounts for the exhilaration that Santayana's letters induce, a sense of the mind suddenly freed, happily disenchanted, active in a new way. Santayana has several times reminded us how close he was to the men of the English late nineteenth century, how great a part Ruskin and Arnold and Pater played in the formation of his thought. What one becomes aware of from the letters is how close he was to the English Romantics. For the kind of mental sensation he imparts is what the Romantic poets thought of as peculiarly appropriate to the mind, and they often represented it by images of the mind "soaring" or on a mountain peak: it was thus that they proposed the escape from the "bondage" of "earth," the ability to move at will in a sustaining yet unresisting medium, the possibility of looking at life in detachment, from a "height." This is a nearly forgotten possibility of the mind; it is not approved by the hidden, prepotent Censor of modern modes of thought. To look within is permitted; to look around is encouraged; but best not to look down—not realistic, not engaged, not democratic. One experiences the unsanctioned altitude with as much guilt as pleasure.

For this pleasure, or the reminder of pleasure, we are of course grateful to Santayana and drawn to him. Yet at the same time there is the easy possibility of disliking him, or at least of regarding him with ready suspicion. It shouldn't matter. It should, indeed, constitute an added charm. Let us just call it "tension" or "ambiguity" or "irony" or whatever name serves to remind us that there is a special intellectual satisfaction in admiring where we do not love, in qualifying our assent, in keeping our distance.

My own antagonism to Santayana goes back to my college days. Irwin Edman, as all his students knew, was a great admirer of Santayana and was said actually to be on terms of friendship with the great man. Edman had an amazing gift as a teacher. He could summarize the thought of a philosopher in a way both to do justice to his subject and to make it comprehensible to the meanest intelligence. Or, if the meanest intelligence didn't actually comprehend, it certainly had the sentiment of comprehension. This I can testify to, because, when it came to philosophy, I was the meanest intelligence going. I found it virtually impossible to know what issues were involved; I could scarcely begin to understand the questions, let alone the answers. But when Edman spoke with that wonderful systematic lucidity of his, all things seemed clear. With, for me, the exception of Santayana. Edman could never make plain to me what Santayana was up to.

If Santayana could now be consulted about why this was so, he would very likely explain that it was because Edman didn't really understand him. He seems to have come to think that no Jew and no Columbia man was likely to understand him. And of course Edman's allegiance to Santayana gradually abated, and in the essay which he contributed to Professor Schilpp's *The Philosophy of George Santayana* he maintains that the later developments of the thought of the man who had been his master verged on the irrelevant and, perhaps, the immoral. And in the reply to his critics which

Santayana makes in the same volume, Santayana permits himself to speak of Edman's objections as showing a "personal animus."

Yet I have no doubt that Edman's account of Santayana was perfectly just and accurate. What stood in the way of my understanding it was a cherished prejudiced. The college group to which I belonged, many of whom were more or less close to Edman, resisted that part of his thought which led him to understand and praise detachment. We were very down on Walter Pater, very hostile to what we called "aestheticism," and we saw Edman's enthusiasm for Santayana as of a piece with his admiration for Pater and as a proof of his mere "aestheticism." I have come to think that Pater is a very remarkable writer, much misrepresented by the critics and literary historians. But at the time we took him to be everything that was disembodied and precious. Santayana seemed to some of us to be in the line of Pater, brought there if only by his prose, which even now I think is only occasionally really good because all too much of it is "beautiful," as the philosophers never weary of telling us. The famous "perfection of rottenness," which William James said that Santayana's thought represented, was wholly apparent to us, and we did not use the phrase with any touch of the admiration that James really did intend.

In short, what Edman (if I read him aright) eventually came to feel about Santayana after a close study of the later work, I felt out of a prejudice based on hearsay. Against this prejudice not even Edman's lucidity and the sympathy he then had with Santayana's mind could make any headway. When an undergraduate entertains a critical prejudice against a literary or philosophical figure, the last person in the world who can change his mind is his teacher.

My case, of course, was not unique. The feeling against Santayana in America is endemic and almost inevitable. It is indeed very difficult for an American, *qua* American—to use the crow-like expression of professional philosophers—to like him or trust him. Of course among the majority of the academic historians of American culture his name is mud. They hustle him off into the limbo they reserve for "aristocratic critics of American democracy." They find it wonderfully convenient to think of him as the "perfection of rottenness" —he is the Gilbert Osmond of their *Portrait of a Lady,* the Lady being America in the perfection of her democracy and innocence: he is a spoiled American, all too elegant, all too cultivated, all too knowing, all too involved with aesthetic values. Actually they are much mistaken. For one thing, Santayana was very severe in his attitude toward the aesthetic experience—as severe as William James and for rather better reasons. This is one of the remarkable and salutary things about him. He was not in the least taken in by the modern pieties about art; and as he grew older art meant less and less to him, and he thought that it should. As for his rejection of America, it is a good deal more complex, not to say cogent, than historians of American culture usually care to remember. America, it is true, seemed to have affected him adversely in an almost physical way, making him anxious and irritable. But it was to a particular aspect of American life that he directed his antagonism, the aspect of what we, with him, may call its gentility, the aspect of its high culture. And what the academic historian of American culture would do without Santayana's phrase "the genteel tradition" is impossible to imagine. Santayana was ill at ease everywhere in America, but what offended his soul was New England, especially Boston, especially Cambridge. For the America of raw energy, the America of material concerns, the America that he could see as young and barbaric and in the line of history he had a tolerance and affection that were real and not merely condescending. Some years ago the late Bernard De Voto raised a storm of protest and contempt among American intellectuals because he wrote in praise of a certain research on the treatment of third-degree burns and insisted that this was a cultural achievement of the first order, that it was an intellectual achievement; he said that it was a fault in American intellectuals that they were not aware of it and did not take pride in it as a characteristic achievement of the American mind. Santayana would have been in agreement with De Voto. In a letter of 1921 to

Logan Pearsall Smith, he writes of high American culture as being ineffectual and sophomoric.

But notice: *all* learning and "mind" in America is not of this ineffectual Sophomoric sort. There is your Doctor at Baltimore who is a great expert, and *really knows how to do things:* and you will find that, in the service of material life, all the arts and sciences are prosperous in America. But it must be in the service of material life; because it is material life (of course with the hygiene, morality, and international good order that can minister to material life) that America has and wants to have and may perhaps bring to perfection. Think of that! If material life could be made perfect, as (in a very small way) it was perhaps for a moment among the Greeks, would not that of itself be a most admirable achievement, like the creation of a new and superior mammal, who would instinctively suck only the bottle? . . . And possibly on that basis of perfected material life, a new art and philosophy would grow unawares, not similar to what we call by those names, but having the same relation to the life beneath which art and philosophy amongst us ought to have had, but never have had actually. You see I am content to let the past bury its dead. It does not seem to me that we can impose on America the task of imitating Europe. The more different it can come to be, the better; and we must let it take its own course, going a long way round, perhaps, before it can shake off the last trammels of alien tradition, and learn to express itself simply, not apologetically, after its own heart.

Here, surely, is the perfect dream, the shaping Whitmanesque principle, of the academic historian of American culture. Santayana, it is true, formulates it with a touch of irony and indeed on another occasion he avowed his belief that everything good in "the ultimate sense" would come to America from Europe only, and from Latin Europe; and of course he was glad that he would not live to see the new American culture come into being. Yet he had too strong a sense of history, too clear an understanding of cultures, not to be as serious as he was ironic.

No, it is not really Santayana's open rejection of America that troubles us about him. His feelings about America go very deep, go to his first principles. That is why they cannot be related to the shabby canting anti-Americanism of the intellectual middle class of

England or of the Continent. A good many things may no doubt be said in dispraise of Santayana, but it cannot be said of him that he had a vulgar mind, that he could possibly think as *The New States-man* thinks. There was no malice in Santayana's feeling about America, nor does he ever give evidence that he had ever been *offended* by America—he had none of the provincial burgher's hurt vengeful pride which led Dostoievski to write *A Winter Diary* to get in his licks at France, or Graham Greene to write *The Quiet American*.

What does alienate Americans from Santayana is the principles upon which his rejection of America is founded. That is, what troubles us is not his negations of America, but the affirmations upon which he based his sense of himself as a European. These disturb us, they put questions to us which we cannot endure.

It isn't possible to speak of Santayana as a representative European. To do so would be to give modern Europe more credit than it deserves. But he was, we might say, the Platonic "idea" of a European. To the development of this idea America was necessary. It was not enough for him to have been Santayana of Avila in Castile; there had also to be the Sturgis connection, and Boston, and Harvard. Santayana repelled the belief that as a boy in Boston he had lived an isolated and unhappy life because he was of foreign birth. He was, he writes, the lieutenant-colonel of the Boston Latin School regiment, he acted in the Hasty Pudding plays at Harvard, he was devoted—"(as a spectator)"—to football. Yet he did stand apart; and he was able to look at the culture into which he had been transplanted with a degree of consciousness that was available to no other lieutenant-colonel and to no other leading lady of a Hasty Pudding play. He knew it to be not his culture, and he lived to develop its opposite principle, the idea of a European culture. This was, to be sure, not monolithically European; England, France, Spain, Italy, Greece were all separate to him, sharp, clear entities which had different values for him at different stages of his life. But, in contrast to America, they came together as a single idea, they made the idea of Europe.

If we ask what it was that Santayana thought of as separating him from America, as making him characteristically and ideally European (and a philosopher), the answer is that it was his materialism. He seems to have found it very difficult to convince people that he really was a materialist. No doubt in his more technical works there are grounds for the resistance to his claim that his materialism was basic to all his thought; of these I have no knowledge. But one reason for the resistance is that we don't expect materialists to compose in highly wrought prose, exquisite and sometimes all too exquisite; we don't expect subtlety and vivacity, supposing, no doubt, that materialists must partake of the dull density of "matter"; we don't expect them to give a very high value to poetry and all fictions, especially the fictions of religions. In 1951 Santayana finds it necessary to write, "Naturalism . . . is something to which I am so thoroughly wedded that I like to call it materialism, so as to prevent all confusion with *romantic* naturalism, like Goethe's, for instance, or that of Bergson. Mine is the hard, non-humanistic naturalism of the Ionian philosophers, of Democritus, Lucretius, and Spinoza." And he goes on: "Those professors at Columbia who tell you that in my *Idea of Christ in the Gospels* I incline to theism have not read that book sympathetically. They forget that my naturalism is fundamental and includes man, his mind, and all his works, products of the generative order of nature."

From Santayana's materialism comes his detachment. Maybe, of course, if we want to look at it psychologically, it is the other way around—the materialism rationalizes the detachment which was temperamental. But certainly the two things go together in Santayana, just as they did in Spinoza, who was perhaps Santayana's greatest hero of thought. The world is matter, and follows the laws of matter. The world is even, he is willing to say, a machine, and follows the laws of its devising. The world is not spirit, following the laws of spirit, made to accommodate spirit, available to full comprehension by spirit. It permits spirit to exist, but this is by chance and chancily: no intention is avowed. And the world, we might go on to say, is Boston to the boy from Avila; the world is the Sturgis family to the young Santayana—not hostile, yet not his own, not continuous with him. It is, as he says, his host, and he must have reflected that the word implies not only a guest but a parasite!

When Bouvard and Pécuchet gave themselves to the study of Spinoza, Flaubert's favorite philosopher, they felt as if they were in "a balloon at night, in glacial coldness, carried on an endless journey towards a bottomless abyss and with nothing near but the unseizable, the motionless, the eternal." We do not feel *quite* this as we read Santayana's letters. They are far too full of intended grace, of conscious charm, too full of the things of this world. But the abyss is there, and his dreadful knowledge of it is what Americans fear in Santayana, just as it is the American avoidance of the knowledge of the abyss that made Santayana fear America and flee it. The knowledge of the abyss, the awareness of the discontinuity between man and the world, this is the forming perception of Santayana's thought as it comes to us in the letters. It is already in force at the age of twenty-three—it makes itself manifest in the perfectly amazing self-awareness and self-possession of the letters he writes from his first trip abroad just after his graduation from Harvard. The philosophical detachment is wholly explicit; and we see at once that it is matched by a personal detachment no less rigorous. For Santayana friendship was always of high special importance. He could be a loyal and devoted friend, as witness his constancy to the unfortunate and erratic Frank Russell, Bertrand Russell's elder brother, his predecessor in the earldom; he could be finely sympathetic as witness his letter to Iris Origo on the death of her only son. But friendship had for him a status in his life like that of art. Art, however lovely, however useful, was not reality; at best it was an element of reality; and sometimes, he said, it interfered with the apprehension of reality. So too he never deceived himself about friendship; its limits were clear to him very early and he never permitted himself to be deceived into thinking that a friend was himself. Nothing could be more striking than Santayana's equal devotion and remoteness in his youthful letters to his friends. He put all his intelligence and all his sympathy at their service, but never himself. It is, in its own way, very fine; but no American reader, I think, can help being made uncomfortable by this stern and graceful self-possession, this rigorous objectivity, this strict limitation, in so very young a man.

And our American discomfort is the more intense, I believe, because we cannot but perceive that Santayana's brilliant youthful reserve is his response to his youthful consciousness of what I have called the abyss. His friend Henry Ward Abbott writes to him out of one of those states of cosmological despair which were common enough among young men even as late as 1887, asking Santayana to consider the problem of life from "the point of view of the grave"; Santayana replies in this fashion:

What you call the point of view of the grave is what I should call the point of view of the easy chair. [That is, the point of view of detached philosophic contemplation.] From that the universal joke is indeed very funny. But a man in his grave is not only apathetic, but also invulnerable. That is what you forget. Your dead man is not merely amused, he is also brave, and if his having nothing to gain makes him impartial his having nothing to lose makes him free. "Is it worth while after all?" you ask. What a simple-hearted question. Of course it isn't worth while. Do you suppose when God made up his mind to create this world after his own image, he thought it was worth while? I wouldn't make such an imputation on his intelligence. Do you suppose he existed there in his uncaused loneliness because it was worth while? Did Nothing ask God before God existed, whether he thought it would be worth while to try life for a while? or did Nothing have to decide the question? Do you suppose the slow, painful, nasty, bloody process, by which things in this world grow, is worth having for the sake of the perfection of a moment? Did you come into the world because you thought it worth while? No more do you stay in it because you do. The idea of demanding that things should be worth doing is a human impertinence.

But then, when Abbott continues the question in a later letter, Santayana says, "The world may have little in it that is good: granted. But that little is really and inalienably good. Its value cannot be destroyed because of the surrounding evil." It is a startling

thing for a youth to say, as startling as his exposition of the point
of view of the grave, and these two utterances may surely be thought
of as definitive of Santayana's later thought. Whatever his materialism leads Santayana to, it does not lead him to a radical relativism
pointing to an ultimate nihilism. It does not lead him to a devaluation of life, to the devaluation of anything that might be valued. On
the contrary—it is the basis of his intense valuation. Here indeed,
we might almost say, is one *intention* of his materialism, that it
should lead to a high valuation of what may be valued at all. If we
are in a balloon over an abyss, let us at least value the balloon. If
night is all around, then what light we have is precious. If there is
no life to be seen in the great emptiness, our companions are to be
cherished; so are we ourselves. And this, I think, is the essence of
the European view of life as it differs from the American. Willa
Cather is not in my opinion a very intelligent or subtle mind, but she
did show in her novels an understanding of the European attachment to *things* and how it differed from the American attachment.
The elaborate fuss that she made about cuisine, about wine, and
salads, and bread, and copper pots, was an expression of her sense
of the unfeeling universe; cookery was a ritual in which the material
world, some tiny part of it, could be made to serve human ends,
could be made human; and in so far as she represents cookery as a
ritual, it is the paradigm of religious belief, and goes along with her
growing sympathy for Catholicism, of which the chief attraction
seemed to be not any doctrinal appeal it had but rather its being *so
very European*. That is, what hope the Catholic religion offered her
took its sanction from the European confrontation of the abyss—the
despair that arises from the knowledge of the material nature of the
world validates all rituals and all fictions that make life endurable
in the alien universe.

If I apprehend Santayana aright, what Miss Cather felt in a very
simple way, he felt in a very elaborate way. That is why he was so
acutely uncomfortable in America. Santayana knew that America
was not materialistic, not in the philosophic sense and not really in

the moral sense. What he says about America's concern with the practical life and with "material well-being" does not contradict this. If anything, it substantiates it.

For if the Americans were truly materialistic, they would recognize the necessity of dualism, they would have contrived a life of the spirit apart from and in opposition to the life of material concern. But for the American consciousness the world is the natural field of the spirit, laid out to be just that, as a baseball diamond or a tennis court is laid out for a particular kind of activity; and what the American wins is not enjoyed as a possession but, rather, cherished as a trophy. The European sees the world as hard and resistant to spirit; whatever can be won is to be valued, protected, used, and enjoyed. But the high valuation of the material life makes, as it were, the necessity for its negation in an intense respect for the life of spirit.

What exasperated Santayana was the American refusal to confront the hard world that materialism proposes, the American preference for seeing the world as continuous with spirit. His animus against Emerson's transcendentalism was extreme, and what he felt about Emerson he felt about all of American philosophic thought, as we see from the brilliant *Character and Opinion in the United States*. The inclusion of the word "character" in that title is significant. One of the things that must especially involve our interest in Santayana's letters is what we perceive to be a chief preoccupation of the writer— the concern for character, for self-definition, for self-preservation. This concern is intimately related to Santayana's materialism. Santayana defined himself in the universe by detachment from it. And what is true of him in the largest possible connection is also true of him in smaller connections. Thus, he had no sooner received his first Harvard appointment than he began to think of the moment when he could retire from Harvard, which he did at the first possible opportunity. It was not merely that he was a foreigner, or that he saw himself as of a different breed from the American academic, or that he could not support what, in an early letter, he calls the "damnable worldliness and snobbishness prevalent at Harvard." It was rather that he needed to define himself by withdrawal.

And how very precise his self-definition is. We see it in the cool self-possession of his dealings with William James. In his early relation with Santayana, James as a teacher is in a very different role from that in which we find him in that all too famous anecdote of Gertrude Stein at Radcliffe, when, to Gertrude Stein's having written nothing in her examination book except the statement that the afternoon was too fine for examinations, James replied with agreement and an A for the course. I have never admired James for this—it seems to me that he gave an unfortunate impetus to all the contemporary student cant about how teachers ought to behave, that, for example, they should be *human*. I like much better James's coming down on Santayana for not having done the conventional thing with his traveling fellowship; I like it in part because it gave Santayana the opportunity to stand up to his superior and to affirm himself and to hold himself ready to take the consequences. And this he does in a way that no American youth could have equaled, with a sincere regard for James, with a perfect if not wholly ingenuous courtesy, with the full sanction of his view of the world, an entire readiness to wipe out his academic career before it should have begun. It isn't exactly endearing; it makes the beginning of our sense that we shall not like Santayana at all. But it is very impressive, it is even very fortifying.

That sense of himself which Santayana shows in his letters to James was what he saw lacking in American life. His novel, *The Last Puritan,* is, as he says, about a man who, with all the personal and material gifts, "peters out," and the tragedy of this he felt to be so terrible that he "actually cried over the writing of it." He speaks of the petering out of most of the young American poets who do not escape to hibernate in Europe. And petering out was, it seems, the fate of most of his Harvard friends—it was not that they were worn out by American life, nor that they were hampered by economic circumstances, or perverted by bad ideals; it was that they did not know how to define themselves, they did not know how to grasp and possess; we might say that they did not know how to break their hearts on the idea of the hardness of the world, to admit the defeat which is requisite for any victory, to begin their effective life in the world by taking the point of view of the grave. Perhaps the whole difference between Santayana and America is summed up in an exchange between him and William Lyons Phelps. No two men could have been more worlds apart than Phelps and Santayana, but Santayana liked Phelps—he was American academic life, and American kindliness, he was all the massive excitement of the Yale-Harvard game, which Santayana relished, making it a point always to stay with the Phelpses whenever the game was in New Haven. When *The Last Puritan* appeared, Phelps was distressed by the book and Santayana had to deal with his objection that he did not "love life" and also with the objection that there were no "good people" in the book. To which Santayana replied, "I don't think you like *good* people, really, only sweet people—like Annabel [Mrs. Phelps] and you!" The sentence seems to me momentous in its definition of American life. In that life sweetness is an endemic trait, and very lovely and valuable it is. But we find it very hard to imagine that definition of character which is necessary to support the strain of what Santayana calls goodness.

As for Santayana himself, his effort of self-definition had, in some ways, an amazing success. He was manifestly not a sweet man, although there are some engagingly kind letters to people whose defenses he knew to be weak, students, young philosophers, old friends who suddenly called themselves to mind after half a century. That he was a good man has been questioned and the question seems to me a very reasonable one—there is certainly something deeply disquieting about his temperament. But there can be no doubt of the firmness of his self-definition; there can be no doubt that he did not peter out. The surrender of hope that he made at an early age, the admission of defeat that many interpret as an essential cynicism or even as a kind of malevolence, may not be life-giving to most of his readers; but it was a regimen that preserved him in life in a way that must astound us. He lived to be nearly ninety, and up to the end there is no intellectual event that he does not respond to with full alertness and full power and full involvement. His comments on Edna St. Vincent Millay make a definitive estimate of her; a few years later he is no less precise about Faulkner. He absorbed Freud far better than most intellectuals, and his essay on *Beyond the Pleasure Principle* deals in a remarkable way with Freud's materialistic assumptions that made Santayana sympathetic to him. He is much interested in the poetry of Robert Lowell, and also in the stories of Somerset Maugham, the point of his interest in the latter being his "wonder at anybody wishing to write such stories." In general he is responsive to the modern element in literature—he is fascinated by Joyce and captivated by Proust; but he says he has no enthusiasm for D. H. Lawrence, Dostoievski, and Nietzsche: he has had from Aristotle, he says, all they can give him. The vivacity and cogency of his mind never abate.

In the letter to Abbott which I quoted earlier he had written that "the point of view of the grave is not to be attained by you or me everytime we happen to want anything in particular. It is not gained except by renunciation. Pleasure must first cease to attract and pain to repel, and this, you will confess, is no easy matter. But meantime, I beg of you, let us remember that the joke of things is one at our expense. It is very funny, but it is exceedingly unpleasant." The ironic smile at the universal joke never left the face of his writing, but neither, I think, did the sense of how unpleasant the joke is. The smile drove philosophers to distraction and led some of them to say that he wasn't a philosopher at all—maybe a poet. "If you took [my lucubrations] more lightly perhaps you would find them less aggravating," he wrote to Professor Lamprecht. He himself thought a smile might say much—in a letter to Father Munson he speaks of the importance in his philosophic life of a passage of Plato's *Parmenides* "about 'ideas' of filth, rubbish, etc., which the moralistic young Socrates recoils from as not beautiful, making old Parmenides smile. That smile of Parmenides made me think." How much for a smile to do! Yet Santayana's does no less.

1956